The Gospel of the FLYING SPAGHETTI MONSTER

BOBBY HENDERSON

VILLARD ⓥ NEW YORK

A Villard Books Trade Paperback Original

Copyright © 2006 by Bobby Henderson

Published in the United States by Villard Books,
an imprint of The Random House Publishing Group,
a division of Random House, Inc., New York.

VILLARD and "V" CIRCLED Design are registered
trademarks of Random House, Inc.

Grateful acknowledgment is made to the following for permission to use
preexisting material:

Kelly Black: Proof entitled "The Case for the Church of the Immaculate
Induction" by Kelly Black. Reprinted by permission of the author.

J. R. Blackwell: Proof entitled "Evidence of the Baker" by J. R. Blackwell.
Reprinted by permission of the author.

Alexis Drummond: Proof entitled "Pirates and Faith" by Alexis Drummond.
Reprinted by permission of the author.

Alexander Gross: Proof entitled "FSM Theologebra" by Alexander Gross.
Reprinted by permission of the author.

Jacob D. Haqq-Misra and Michael B. Larson: Proof entitled "Piracy as a
Preventor of Tropical Cyclones" by Jacob D. Haqq-Misra and Michael B.
Larson. Reprinted by permission of the authors.

Kevin Heinright: Proof entitled "A Twenty-first-Century Ontological
Argument" by Kevin Heinright. Reprinted by permission of the author.

James Hofer: Proof entitled "Mathematical Proof of the FSM" by James
Hofer. Reprinted by permission of the author.

Toby Leonard: Proof entitled "Of Penguins and Pasta" by Toby Leonard
with editing by Jason Braunwarth. Reprinted by permission of the author.

Nick Moran: Proof entitled "Life, Kolgoromov Complexity, and Delicious
Spaghetti" by Nick Moran. Reprinted by permission of the author.

Landon W. Rabern: Proof entitled "A Teleological Argument" by Landon W.
Rabern. Reprinted by permission of the author.

Scott Stoddard: Proof entitled "A Corporate Proof of the Flying Spaghetti
Monster" by Scott Stoddard. Reprinted by permission of the author,
www.thefourthrow.blogspot.com.

ISBN 0-8129-7656-8

Printed in the United States of America

www.villard.com

9 8 7

In the beginning was the Word,
and the Word was "Arrrgh!"

—PIRATICUS 13:7

Acknowledgments

DELIVERING A DIVINE MESSAGE requires a great deal of coordination and effort on the part of many people. I would like to acknowledge the hard work of all those who have devoted long hours and considerable mind power to keeping up the website and thereby assuring that His Word is spread across the globe. To you all, I say, thank you from the bottom of my heart—you have done benevolent and thoughtful work, and together we have accomplished much, though I can't help feeling that our greatest moments are still ahead of us.

To my agent, Paula Balzer, I offer my sincerest gratitude. You have been brave and steadfast, guiding me through occasionally stormy seas like the great Pirate that you are.

This book could never have happened without the unwavering dedication of the publishing crew at Villard. Thank you to Daniel Menaker, editor in chief of Random House, for his wisdom, vision, and encouragement. Thank you to Sanyu Dillon and Avideh Bashirrad for their kindness and support, and especially for the marketing genius that helped get this book off to a great start. Thank you to Erich Schoeneweiss for producing a great book and contributing his own Piratical ideas on many an occasion. Thank you to Simon Sullivan and Gabe Levine for their incredible design. Thank you to Nancy Delia for her patience and unwavering commitment to this project. Thank you to Tim Mak, who is an artist, gentleman, and Pirate all in one. And, above all, my greatest thanks goes to my editor, Chris Schluep, without whom the Flying Spaghetti Monster wouldn't even have gotten off the ground. I nominate you official Pastriarch of FSMism.

RAmen.

Contents

Disclaimer

WHILE PASTAFARIANISM IS the only religion based on empirical evidence, it should also be noted that this is a faith-based book. Attentive readers will note numerous holes and contradictions throughout the text; they will even find blatant lies and exaggerations. These have been placed there to test the reader's faith.

Disclaimer About Midgets[1]

OUR RELIGION DOES NOT WISH to discriminate or cause hurt feelings among any group—and this is especially true of the very short, who, if provoked, could easily appear out of nowhere and attack. As a solution, we offer the following:

To prevent angering the little people community, we suggest that this book be placed on the very highest shelf possible.

1. Sometimes referred to as "midgits" or "little people."

DEAR FRIEND,

Welcome to the wonderful world of religion!

These are exciting times in holiness—politicians are crusading, nations are invading, and science[1] is fading. With these changes come religious opportunities the likes of which haven't been seen since the Reformation . . . or at least since the persecuted masses first huddled together and shipped off to that great democratic revival meeting we call the United States of America.

With this in mind, the Church of the Flying Spaghetti Monster (FSM) invites you to learn a little more about us. We'd like to tell you all about our Heaven, which features a Stripper Factory and a giant Beer Volcano. We'd love to see you dressed in His chosen garb: full Pirate regalia. We want you to enjoy Fridays as His chosen holiday. But first you need to know a little more about us.

What do we stand for?

- *All that is good.*

What are we against?

- *All that isn't good.*

Sounds sweet, right? Of course it's not that simple, and that's why we need a book. (Doesn't every religion have a book?) The Jews have the Bible (The Old Testicle), the Christians have ditto (The New Testicle), the Muslims have the Q-tip or whatever, the Jains have Fun with Dick and Jain, the Sufis have Sufis Up!, the Buddhists have the Bananapada, the Hindus have Ten Little Indians, the Wiccans have The Witches of Eastwick, and so on. If this was a manifesto, a pamphlet, a flyer, an

1. Also known as the language of the forked tongue.

2. Also known as "Pastafari-anism."

article, or some nut preaching from a street corner, you, fair reader, might perceive FSMism[2] to be just another two-bit cult. But we're not a cult (we're more like a boutique religion at this point), and this is a book that will stand up to any of the others—at least in terms of strict plausibility if not literary finesse and retributive beheadings and disembowelments. The more you read about us the more you're going to be persuaded that the Flying Spaghetti Monster is the *true* Creator and that FSMism just might be the Best. Religion. Ever.

Go ahead. Try us for thirty days. If you don't like us, your old religion will most likely take you back. Unless it's the Jains, whose feelings are easily hurt.

RAmen.

BOBBY HENDERSON
Prophet

THE BLUNDERS OF SCIENCE

*Part of education is to expose people
to different schools of thought.*

—GEORGE W. BUSH, closet Pastafarian

The Need for Alternative Theories

SCIENCE IS A SUBJECT IN CRISIS. There's a dirty little secret that the scientific establishment has been trying to keep under wraps for years: There are many unproven theories that are being taught to people as if they were established fact. But thanks to the heroic efforts of a handful of deep thinkers, the winds of truth are sweeping across the nation.

Consider the theory of Evolution. To their credit, Intelligent Design advocates have successfully argued that their alternative theory deserves as much attention as Evolution, since neither can be considered fact. This is a valid point, but Evolution is hardly the only theory in trouble.

It seems strange that Evolution is singled out as "just a theory" when there are so many basic ideas in science that remain unproven, yet are still taught as fact. The objections to teaching Evolution have only illustrated this point further: *Alternative theories must be taught in order to give our young students' minds a broad foundation.* The Intelligent Design proponents make a compelling, and totally legitimate, argument that if a theory has not been proven, then one suggested theory is just as good as another.

Take gravity, for example: the force of attraction between massive particles. We know a great deal about the properties of gravity, yet we know nothing about the cause of the force itself. Why are particles attracted to one other? If we review the literature, we find a lot of material dealing with the properties of gravity, but very little dealing with the underlying cause of this attraction. Until we have a proven answer to this question, it seems irresponsible to instruct students in what is, ultimately, just a theory. However, if we must discuss the theory of gravity at all, then it's reasonable that all suggested theories should be given equal time, since none have been proven or disproven. Therefore, I formally submit that the Flying Spaghetti Monster is behind this strange and often misunderstood force.

What if it is He, pushing us down with His Noodly Appendages, that causes this force? He is invisible, remember, and is undetectable by current instruments, so in theory it is possible. And the fact that the gravitational powers of the Spaghetti Monster haven't been disproven makes it all the more likely to be true. We can only guess as to His motives, but it's logical to assume that if He is going to such trouble, there is a good reason. It could be that He doesn't want us floating off earth into space, or maybe just that He enjoys touching us—we may never know.[1]

And while it's true that we don't have any empirical evidence to back up this theory, keep in mind the precedent set by Intelligent Design proponents. Not only is observable, repeatable evidence not required to get an alternative theory included in the curriculum, but simply poking holes in established theory may be enough. In this case, the established theory of gravity makes no mention as to the *cause* of the force; it merely presents the properties of it. I fully expect, then, that this FSM theory of gravity will be admitted into accepted science with a minimum of apparently unnecessary bureaucratic nonsense, including the peer-review process.

For further evidence of the true cause of gravity—that we are being pushed down by His Noodly Appendages—we need only look at our historical records. The average height of humans two thousand years ago was about five feet three inches for males, compared with an average height of around five feet ten inches for males today. Useless by itself, this information becomes quite important when viewed in terms of worldwide population. Humans, apparently obsessed with fucking, have increased their numbers exponentially over the years. We find, counterintuitively, that a small population correlates with shorter humans, and a larger population correlates with taller humans.[2] This only makes sense in light of the FSM theory of gravity. With more people on earth today, there are fewer Noodly Appendages to go around, so we each receive less touching—pushing down toward the earth—and thus, with less force downward, we're taller.

We can fully expect that as the population increases, and we receive

1. It would appear that midgets receive the most FSM touching—thus placing them on a pedestal in His eyes.

2. If we are to believe that height is a function of nutrition, as we're told, then a smaller population with more food available per person should correlate to a taller height. This is not what we find.

EARLY MAN: SHORT

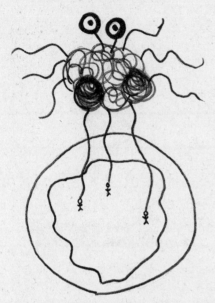

MODERN MAN: TALL

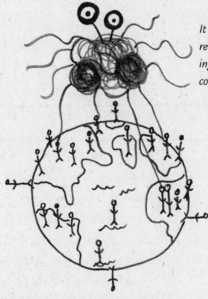

It is evident that early man received much more touching than his modern-day counterparts.

less downward pushing by the FSM, we'll continue to grow in height. Conversely, we can expect that the sudden occurrence of a worldwide plague would cause our average height to decrease. This phenomenon can be verified in historical records. We find that regions undergoing health crises have shorter people—strong evidence that the theory is sound.

No one is saying that the FSM theory of gravity is necessarily true, but at the very least, it's based on sound science, sound enough to be included in the curriculum with the other nonproven theories. Until the currently taught theory of gravity, known as Newtonism, is proven as fact, alternatives should be taught as well.

The unusually high placement of this prehistoric cave art is attributed to the natural shelter that caves provided from His Noodly Appendages.

An Alternative Viewpoint

A Note from
Ferris P. Longshanks: *County Sheriff, School Board Member, Concerned Citizen*

Honestly, fellow citizens, I don't understand what all the fuss is about. We're not saying that Intelligent Design is any more valid than Evolution or any other half-baked theory of creation—all we're interested in is giving people *choices*.

Isn't that what America is all about?

Republican *or* Democrat
McDonald's *or* Burger King
Target *or* Wal-Mart
Coke *or* Pepsi

And here's another to consider . . .

The Benevolent Lord Our Savior *or*
Everlasting Damnation in Hellfire

Whichever side you fall on doesn't really matter, because we're *all* Americans. Still, any real American supports his or her inalienable right to have choices—and lots of 'em. For what are people without choices? Communists! And despite this fact, there are those who would bar the public from having an open and honest discussion about Intelligent Design, a scientific concept that's so clear and logical as to appeal to Baptist holy men and intellectually discerning NASCAR fans alike.

Sometimes I see the hypocrisy and just shake my head.

Granted, these are controversial issues we're dealing with, and well-reasoned people do disagree on whether life as we know it was created by a benevolent and all-knowing Creator (ID)—or through a random and heartless struggle for dominance, commonly known as survival of the fittest (Evolution).

For the sake of clarity, allow me to use a simple analogy to explain these two very different versions of creation.

Say you want to buy one of those new flatscreen TVs that are so popular these days. According to the opposing theories of ID and Evolution, you might acquire that TV in two very different ways:

1. You could assume, quite fairly, that Intelligent Designers from Sony, Toshiba, and Sharp are actively producing new and affordable forty-two-inch, high-definition flatscreen TVs, which are then boxed and shipped to the nearest Wal-Mart or Circuit City for you to purchase. Or . . .
2. You could wait several million years for a new flatscreen TV to *evolve spontaneously* from a "soup" composed of mud, DNA, and spare television parts. Once this happens, you might attempt to drag your new television out of a swamp and back to your house (or more likely, cave) before a stranger comes swinging out of a tree, kills you and your children, then inseminates your wife with his own seed.

As you can see, both theories present potentially dramatic conse-quences for society. I'm not saying that one scenario is more valid than the other, but I will say that the Intelligent Design option is the first one. In the interest of fairness, I'll also say that Evolution (or

Natural Selection) is the one where your wife gets raped by a man who lives in a tree. Both theories present unique challenges.

When considering the two, ask yourself which makes more sense in your life.

Then ask yourself, Who's making these arguments, anyway?

ID proponents can boast of *several* scientists—brave men who are willing to be called upon by name—to represent their views. You've seen these pro-ID champions on your televisions (which, we can safely assume, were designed by engineers and bought from a store . . .

Dead.

further proof). You've observed them being viciously attacked by activist judges, the liberal media, and a certain Bobby Henderson. But where are the men of science who speak out in support of Evolution?

A number of scientists have been cited in defense of Evolution, but if we examine the situation more closely we begin to see a disturbing pattern.

Names like Darwin, Einstein, Carl Sagan, Stephen Jay Gould, Ernst Meyer—and many other scientists who 95 percent of the country have never heard of—are offered up as men who've supported Evolution. Yet you've never seen one of these so-called scientists publicly defending their theory. Why?

Answer: Because they're all *dead*.

Hmm . . . coincidence? When the pro-Evolutionary movement has to resort to dead scientists (who are probably a little warm right now, if you get my drift), it makes one wonder how good an argument they actually have. What's next . . . bringing back Aristotle (a homosexual) and Ptolemy (forgotten) to argue for a flat earth? Given the pro-Evolutionists' track record, that can't be too far away.

As I've stated, we do see living judges trying to wield their laws in the face of this highly scientific discussion. However, I predict that the well-prepared ID scientists will soon have liberal activist judges quaking in their penny loafers. These judges are much better suited for sanctioning same-sex marriage, and most of them are old and easily confused. Ignore their words and proclamations, for they tire easily.

The liberal media has also chimed in on the subject, only to be reminded that they're just overpromoted weathermen with good hair, deep voices, and small penises. I don't have conclusive evidence on this last point, but looking at Stone Phillips I'm pretty sure it's true. Don't worry about the media, they'll lose interest as soon as forest fire season returns.

Aside from dead scientists, activist judges, and the liberal media, one other man has arisen as a voice for the Evolutionists—if not necessarily to argue for Evolution, then at least to mock the ID movement. We know little about this man, who hails from the Pacific Northwest and calls himself "Bobby Henderson."

Far be it from me to cast stones, but there are disturbing rumors about him going around. I read on the Internet that he's not even a scientist. Also, a very reliable source reports that he lied about his military record. I hear that he's been divorced three times and sleeps in a crypt. Not all of these rumors are verified, but if we're to let this lying divorcé, who may or may not be a shape-shifting night creature, take a lead on this important debate, I can only pray for the redemption of this country.

In conclusion, I would like to return to my original argument: We the People need *choices*. We need as many choices as possible, and we can't allow the leftist cabal of scientists, judges, Bobby Henderson, and the media to take these choices away from us. Write your congressmen and demand that ID be taught in the schools. Write your religious leaders and demand that they write your congressmen.

If we don't act now, I fear the day will come when judges and the media are free to operate with little regard for the tempering hand of public outrage. Laws will be passed and upheld, and only judges will be able to rule on them. The media will report the news without threat of subpoena. To put it bluntly, the god-hating communists will have finally won.

I wonder if they'll appoint Bobby Henderson to be their dictator.

Toward a New SuperScience

WE ARE ENTERING INTO AN EXCITING TIME, when no longer will science be limited to natural explanations. Who is to say that there aren't supernatural forces—magic, some might call it—at work, controlling events around us? Propelled by popular opinion and local government, science is quickly becoming receptive to all logical theories, natural and supernatural alike. Not since the Middle Ages have we seen such open-minded science policy.

What is science, really? Some might call it the observational, descriptive, experimental, and theoretical explanation of phenomena. And so, not surprisingly, there are a few who argue that supernatural theories have no place in science, since they make no testable claims about the world. But that idea is a little shortsighted. Science is also a collection of tools whose purpose is to enable mankind to solve problems. In this sense, supernatural—or magic, metaphysical, not real, what have you— theories have the potential to be just as helpful, if not more helpful, than the standard natural-only science we've used for the last two hundred years.

Extending the science tool metaphor further, shouldn't we endeavor to give scientists the largest collection of tools possible? No one is saying that they have to apply a supernatural explanation to any particular phenomenon, only that the supernatural be available if nothing else works, or if it is convenient for deceptive political purposes. And remember, this is not a radical new idea. In terms of years in use, supernatural science—SuperScience, if you will—has the edge on conventional science. Conventional, or empirical, science has been in use for only a few hundred years. Obviously there must be a reason supernatural science lasted so long, before this empirical-science fad began. Could it be that supernatural science is more productive than empirical science?

Consider the discovery and development of new land, an important scientific pursuit by anyone's standard. If we compare a period of time in which supernatural science was the norm—say the years A.D. 1400[1] to 1600, to a period of time in which empirical science was preferred—say the years 1800 to 2000—we can get a clear picture of just how detrimental empirical science can be.

1. Al dente.

LAND AREA DISCOVERED

SUPERNATURAL SCIENCE	EMPIRICAL SCIENCE
Years 1400–1600	*Years 1800–2000*
14.5 million sq km	0.3 million sq km

Here, empirical science comes up short even with every technological advantage it possesses. Even with satellite imagery and GPS navigation, scientists bound by the chains of empiricism have been unable to discover even a paltry 3 percent of the amount of new land that their supernatural-science counterparts found in an equal period of time. Scientists and explorers in the years 1400–1600 had few maps, only a compass, cross-staff, or astrolabe for navigation, and no motorized transportation. Yet even with these setbacks, they still managed to discover more than 14 million square kilometers of new, developable land. Clearly their openness to supernatural forces had something to do with their success, and we can only guess that they were guided to these new-

found lands by some creature—most likely the Flying Spaghetti Monster, as historical art suggests.

It's only logical to assume that returning to balanced methods of science—natural theories and supernatural theories both—would allow us to find more land, something we greatly need for our growing population. More land means more resources, and more resources means fewer starving children. I can safely say, then, that anyone against the inclusion of supernatural theories into science wants children to starve. Such people obviously have no place in policymaking, and so I suggest that they get no say on the issue.

Next, we'll look at medicine. It might seem crazy to claim that medicine was superior in the Middle Ages—when science included the su-

The Italian explorer Christopher Columbus was guided by a Higher Power.

pernatural—than it is today—being now limited to the study of natural phenomena—but let's take a closer look. Medieval medicine was dominated by religion, and yes, sickness was generally thought to be punishment for sins, and so treatment then consisted mainly of prayer. But let's not forget about the "antiquated" medical procedures that were ultimately so successful as to render them unnecessary today.

Bloodletting, the removal of considerable amounts of blood from a patient's body, is considered heinous by today's supposedly superior doctors, but who is to say that the procedure didn't do more good than modern medicine? Medical texts from the Middle Ages—anyone with even a moderate understanding of Latin can read them, and we have no reason to doubt their validity—tell us that many ailments, from headaches to cancer, are the result of evil spirits who are angry with us. We now know, of course, that there are many causes for these ailments, not just spirits at work, but it's clear from the texts that they were a very significant cause of sickness—one that does not exist today, because bloodletting worked so well as to defeat these sickness spirits completely, much the same way polio was cured with high doses of vitamin C. To those who disagree, let me ask you: When was the last time you suffered a demon-induced fever?

But there are more diseases out there, and it's apparent that medical science, equipped with only modern methods, cannot defeat them all. Why not, then, give these doctors and scientists more tools and the flexibility to consider supernatural causes as well as natural ones? Who knows what other ailments, even non-demon-induced ones, might be cured with a simple bloodletting or application of leeches? We'll never know until we try.

And while it's true that many people believe in the power of prayer to cure disease, there's never been any verifiable evidence to support the practice. That's not to say it's not possible—it certainly is possible that prayer aids in healing—but it could very well be that these prayers are being applied in a nonoptimal fashion, thus explaining the lack of evidence for their effectiveness. The truth is we don't know because current scientific methods and religious sensitivities don't allow this type of study. What if those praying are simply praying to the wrong God, or offending Him somehow? What if, by the wearing of a simple eye patch or Pirate bandanna, those praying might have their prayers answered by the FSM?

History is full of examples of supernatural events, and unless we are saying that we're somehow more intelligent and educated, better equipped to understand unexplained events today than we were five hundred years ago, then we must accept the explanations given to these events by those who witnessed them. Witches, for example, existed in such quantity and caused so much trouble that it was necessary to hunt them down and burn them in the tens of thousands. Here it is, the twenty-first century, hundreds of years later, plenty of time for the population of witches to have grown exponentially, yet they are decidedly less of a problem now than they were half a millennia ago. I have never even *seen* a witch, let alone felt the need to burn one to death. We can conclude, then, that our forefathers, equipped with the knowledge that supernatural explanations were reasonable, rounded up all the witches in existence and took care of them.

The other possibility is that there are witches out there, hiding somewhere, plotting their revenge, liberally applying fireproofing compounds to themselves. And someday they may reappear and start causing trouble. And then what will our high and mighty scientists do? Throw calculators at them? Witches eat calculators. The scientific community will be helpless to defeat the threat of these witches, offering only "logical" and "reasoned" explanations for the horrible events the witches are magically inflicting on us.

Witch eating a calculator.

We tend to exalt our rigid empirical methods and technological advances, almost as if we're proud of what we've accomplished with them, but when the record clearly shows that supernatural, nonempirical science produces these kinds of results—the discovery of new lands, the elimination of demon-inducing illnesses, and the extinction of witches—it's time to rethink our methods and return to what gave us *real* results.

The biggest irony is that the arguments given *against* the inclusion of supernatural theories in the realm of accepted science actually *show clearly* that supernatural theories are legit fields of scientific study. No one is saying that empirical, natural-only science and supernatural science can't live side by side. They can, and in fact, they must. Intelligent design may shun natural explanations for phenomena, but FSMism makes use of both the natural and the supernatural equally.

FSMism

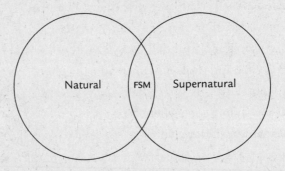

INTELLIGENT DESIGN

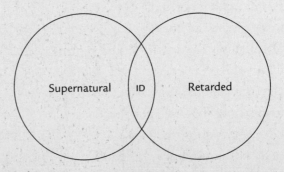

What's the Matter with Evolution?

Highlighting the Problem

WE HEAR A LOT ABOUT EVOLUTION these days. Scientists seem to have embraced the subject as though it were the Second Coming of ... well ... science. But where has it gotten us? Are we to believe that just because we're descended from a common ancestor shared with monkeys, dogs, or whatever, that we understand our situation on this earth any better than we would without Evolution to guide us? Is Evolution going to somehow make my life more satisfying? Can Evolution put food on my table? Will it save the earth from global warming?

The answer to all of the above is a big No. And why is that? Because Evolution is about as useful as a screen door on a submarine. Sure, scientists while away their days trying to devise this or that proof to show that Evolution is a credible idea, but as long as it's *just a theory*, no one in the real world is going to take it seriously. So I've decided to do some debunking of my own to show the world that the big, bad scientists aren't "all that," as the kids like to say.

What is Evolution but the gradual change of species over a lengthy period of time as a result of various internal and external selective pressures? My grandfather, who is as old as dirt, has been through that. According to early lithographs, he was quite a looker in his day, but now, a century later, after years of hard drinking and working in the mines, he has no hair and looks like shit. Could Evolution just mean *growing old*? I posed this question to a scientist friend who explained that the change has to take place over many generations. You'd think the Evolutionists would have stated that right out front, and I admit that I stand corrected. But Evolution still sounds a lot like growing old to me, and I can't help thinking that this is where the Evolutionary scientists first got their wacky ideas.

Having cleared up this common confusion, let us move on to the proposed selective force of Evolution—namely, *Natural Selection*. What the fuck is this supposed to mean? Is there unnatural selection? And who's doing the selecting? Neither of these questions could be answered by my scientist friend, and so I have been forced to ditch my now former friend and perform my own research. What follows is, to the best of my ability, what I've been able to uncover regarding Evolution and Natural Selection.

A Closer Examination of Natural Selection

Apparently, there are not one but two forms of selection. They are Natural Selection and sexual selection. I'll let you mull over the second "sexy" form of selection for a minute, at least until I've torn the first one to shreds. You should have time to masturbate while reading my proofs, if that's what you're in to.

According to the neo-Darwinists, most Evolutionary change is attributable to Natural Selection, meaning that individuals carrying genes that are better suited to their environment will leave more offspring than individuals carrying genes that make them less adaptive. Over time, these more adaptive traits will proliferate, altering the genetic composition of the overall population, since individuals with better "fitness"[1] pass more of their genes into the next generation. It is this process, scientists will tell you, that produced the platypus, the penguin, and the poodle—leading us to conclude that scientists are definitely full of shit. If someone can explain to me the adaptive traits of the "duckbill," then they can certainly tell me why the platypus is the *only mammal on the planet* that has one? Are platypii (pusses . . . who knows?) concerned with ingratiating themselves into local duck populations? Do they think that they're funny? Why the fuck do they have a bill?

I'll take it easy on the scientists regarding the platypus, because obviously it's a tough one, but I'm sure there are several hundred scientists right now earning their tenure in a pointless search for the Evolutionary significance of this ridiculous creature. I'll close on the platypus by

1. "Fitness" regards how well individuals "fit" in their environment.

stating an alternative theory that I've come up with: the Flying Spaghetti Monster made the platypus because, unlike scientists, He has a sense of humor. It's an unlikely sign from God—and until someone can prove me wrong, that's my theory.

I will next turn to more ordinary and boring examples of Natural Selection, which I will then proceed to slice to ribbons. Let us look at the fascinating case of bacteria. It is well known that antibiotics are used to cure various illnesses caused by bacteria, and it is equally well known that most bacteria (for example, staphylococci)[2] eventually develop immunity to these antibiotics. Looking a little closer at the case of staphylococci, we find that, in 1929, Sir Alexander Fleming[3] first observed the bacterium staphylococci to experience inhibition on an agar plate contaminated by a penicillium[4] mold. Sir Alexander Fleming, or "F-Man" as the queen liked to call him, isolated the penicillium to make penicillin, which then went on to be known as a wonder drug for many diseases, mainly VD. But gradually penicillin in its natural form became useless. Scientists will tell you that the bacterium—which replicates faster than a chinchilla in a Cialis factory—eventually developed a strain of itself that was resistant to naturally formed penicillin, and that the process of Natural Selection caused this resistant strain to propagate in nature. This is an outright lie, which I will decimate momentarily.

If we look at bacteria that grow resistant to antibiotics, insects that grow resistant to DDT, or even HIV that grows resistant to antiviral drugs, we see a fascinating correlation between "Natural Selection" and "resistance." But what are we really seeing here? I submit that they're not changing their genetic makeup, they're changing their *minds*. In short, they're getting smarter. If I go to your house and you feed me a shit sandwich two days in a row, I'm having lunch at McDonald's on the third day. It's that simple. Don't let the scientists, with their big phallic bacterial names, tell you anything different. They're not as smart as they pretend to be, no matter how much they try to demean so-called lower life forms.

2. Most scientists are perverted and use Latinate terms to hide this fact. Translated into English, staphylococci means "Power Penis."

3. No relation to Sir Elton John.

4. Meaning "many tiny penises."

One other example of Natural Selection should just about put this puppy to bed. Scientists have pointed to "artificial selection" to show that humans, by providing their own specific set of selective forces, can mimic the forces of nature. We see this over and over again in the actions of "breeders," who purportedly have wrought immense changes in plants and animals. We can look to the various breeds of dogs as an example, where claims are made that all dog species originated from one common source: the ancestral wolf. From this ferocious beast we are expected to believe that a diverse assortment of species was created by man himself—such four-legged brutes as the Chihuahua, the dachshund, the poodle, and the bulldog—all of which have been with us since time immemorial. This breeding "myth" appears to be a form of propaganda, possibly put forth by anti–Intelligent Design campaigners, although I'll save any conversation about Intelligent Design for a later chapter. How can we believe such claims about "man's best friend" when it is obvious to the common observer that every breed has been put on this planet *to serve a purpose*. I, for one, would point to the FSM as the creator of dogs, although there is valid evidence that God (if he is ever proven to exist) might have had a hand in their creation. After all, aren't German shepherds meant to provide us with protection, maybe even from their own "forefathers," the wolf?[5] Weren't poodles and Chihuahuas put on this earth to make us feel better about ourselves? There can be little doubt that an intelligent creator put all the species on earth to serve man. And Evolution wasn't even properly invented until the late 1800s. Is that enough time to get a Labrador retriever from a dire wolf? I think not.

If you don't buy this argument, consider this one last example, which in this case regards plant species. If we look at domestic cabbage, broccoli, kale, cauliflower, and brussels sprouts, are we to claim, even if they did originate from a common ancient wild cabbage, that selection, be it natural, artificial, whatever, could not have done better over the last few thousand years? The answer is written in the squinched-up face of every child with a brussels sprout in his or her mouth. Yet another strike against Evolution.

5. See various stories by Jack London.

Not in a million fucking years . . .

From Pirates to People

Any discussion of Evolution will eventually lead us to ourselves. Humans have been around for as long as we can remember, and yet the Evolutionists will tell you that we weren't. They will tell you that humans and chimpanzees shared a common ancestor some five million years ago, and that we "diverged" from that common ancestor and eventually invented the space shuttle while chimpanzees were only able to invent "the stick." To support this thesis, scientists tell us that we share 95 percent of our DNA with chimpanzees, and yet we share 99.9 percent of our DNA with Pirates.[6] I ask you, who is the more likely common ancestor? And are the Pirates not the Chosen People of the FSM? Why do we spend so much time talking about something that didn't happen, while the FSM is dangling His Noodly Appendage right in front of our faces?

But I shall persevere just a little further, and I shall examine the human body—specifically, I will examine organs that have been deemed "vestigial," or useless, as a result of losing their function over millennia of Evolution.

6. I find it suspicious that biology textbooks rarely mention this fact.

A more credible theory.

Wisdom Teeth

Fallacy: Emerging in adulthood, these teeth are thought to have served as extra grinding surfaces for early man, who, before the advent of proper dental care, would most likely have lost many of his teeth by his mid-twenties.[7]

Fact: It is common knowledge that our Pirate ancestors ate a diet much rougher and more manly than our diets today. Also, they tended to carry their knives set deep in the back of their mouths.[8] It is logical, then, that they'd need extra teeth.

7. Wisdom teeth appear to still serve a useful function in parts of the Deep South.

8. See Robert Louis Stevenson's *Treasure Island*.

Male Nipples

Fallacy: Scientists believe that all humans had breasts—or "dugs"—back in the Stone Age.

Fact: Male nipples were used by Pirates as portable weather stations. With their nipples they were able to determine the direction of the trade winds and, depending on stiffness, how cold it was outside.

"Looks like we're gonna get a nor'easter."

Goose Bumps

Fallacy: Evolutionary propaganda would have you believe that goose bumps are an atavistic, now useless response to distress—be it emotional or weather-related—that was once meant to raise the hair on our early forefathers, causing them to appear larger and scarier.

Fact: Goose bumps are a cleverly disguised feature that allowed for increased buoyancy once a Pirate hit cold water. By simply appearing, they raised the surface area, thus increasing buoyancy. This made Pirates float better—something that was very useful to our ancestors, as they were sometimes without boats. Naturally, goose bumps seem to be a vestigial reflex, but it's really society that has changed.

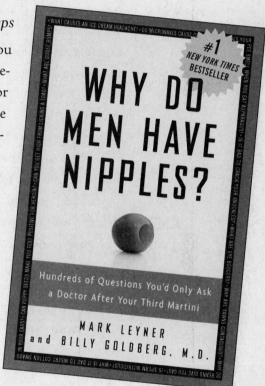

Appendix

Fallacy: This is a remnant of an internal pouch used to ferment the hard-to-digest plant diets of our ancestors.

Fact: The appendix was a clever internal pouch utilized for hiding a Pirate's gold. It is also the inspiration for the saying "cough it up," which Pirates would demand of defeated Pirates once they'd boarded their ships.

Tailbone

Fallacy: Evolutionists claim that the tailbone, or coccyx, which has no documented use, is an unusual remnant of a larger bone growth that might once have formed an ancestral tail, homologous to the functional tails of other primates.

Fact: Humans with tails . . . are scientists high? Couldn't the coccyx have served other purposes? I have carefully researched this issue, and have compared the coccyx to other unusual bone growths in animals—and the literature has led me to a single, overriding conclusion. Lots of animals have horns on their heads, and these aren't thought to be the remnants of larger bone growth, probably because, unlike the coccyx, horns serve a purpose today. But what if the original purpose of the coccyx has simply been rendered useless by today's culture? If you examine the coccyx closely you will see that this bony growth is very similar, when you think about it, to a *horn*, which is the structure used by many animals for fighting. I submit, then, that the coccyx is not a vestige of an ancestral tail but rather an effective, albeit strangely placed, defense and fighting mechanism.

I imagine that two opponents, fighting over women or choice cave real estate, would have run backward at each other—their asses outstretched, much the way elk fight with their horns. I have termed this ass-fighting. This makes sense, if you think about it, as it would leave their hands free to carry whatever they needed—most likely food or rocks.

As further evidence that the coccyx is a fighting feature, and that some knowledge of its use has survived culturally through the years, consider how quickly someone will run away from you if you run at them backward, ass first. I suggest that those who doubt this hypothesis put it to the test, and attempt to ram their ass into everyone they see for the next few days.[9] I feel confident that most, if not all, of these targets will at the very least be afraid. I see no other explanation for why this would occur, other than that we know, subconsciously, that the coccyx is a weapon, not a vestigial tail.

9. Women are not advised to try this in the company of perverted men.

One Other Vestigial Feature

Fallacy: The human genome provides evidence that we humans were not created ex nihilo,[10] but instead had to evolve systematically, just like all the other animals. As evidence, scientists point to lots of nonfunctional DNA, including many inactive "pseudo genes" that were functional in some of our ancestors but aren't today. One example that is often cited is the case of vitamin C synthesis. While all primates, including humans, carry the gene responsible for synthesizing vitamin C, that gene is inactive in all members of the primate family but one: man. Scientists point to this as evidence of our shared lineage, although I can't figure out why.

Fact: Pirates, our ancestors, lived in the tropics and ate a lot of fruit.

10. Nihilos were an early Roman snack food, an early predecessor to Doritos. Essentially, this term translates to "from Doritos."

Evolution Gets Sexy

Finally, I will address "sexual selection," which I promised some time earlier. The basic concept behind sexual selection is that one gender of the species, usually the female, actively chooses members of the opposite sex to copulate with,[11] based on certain criteria, thus placing a selective pressure on the species as a whole. Sexual selection explains the bright foliage of male birds, the impressive ritualistic duels among male rams, deer, elk, and other ungulates,[12] and the high percentage of Hummers being driven by short, ugly men. In short, sexual selection depends on the success of certain individuals over others of the same sex, while Natural Selection is *non-gender specific*. In the interest of modernity, I move that Congress pass a bill outlawing this backward and sexist practice.

11. Fuck.

12. Rams, deer, elk, etc.

The Spaghedeity

While I have essentially decimated the theory of Evolution throughout these pages, it is important to state that a great deal of credible Evolutionary evidence does exist. No one can dispute the fossil record, which shows a clear and gradual transformation of species over time (albeit with frustrating gaps—and I ask you, Who could have put *them* there?). And there do indeed appear to be selective forces at work in the world, for instance when drunks walk out onto the road and are hit by cars.[13]

13. Also, George W. Bush bears a striking resemblance to a chimpanzee.

We are not saying that Evolution *can't* exist, only that it is guided by His Noodly Appendage. And our Spaghedeity is extremely modest. For some reason, He went through a great deal of trouble to make us believe that Evolution is true—masking the prominent role of Pirates in our origins, making monkeys seem more important than they really are, generally keeping behind the scenes and out of the spotlight.

In spite of His low profile, though, let no one doubt that the Church of the Flying Spaghetti Monster is not only a groundbreaking religion, but is also supported by hard science, making it probably the most unquestionably true theory ever put forth in the history of mankind. To make my point, I will turn to the modern-day problem of global warming.

Pirates, as you know, are His Chosen People. Yet their numbers have been shrinking ever since the 1800s. Consequently, we find that global warming, earthquakes, hurricanes, and other natural disasters are a direct result of the shrinking number of Pirates. To illustrate this fact, I have included the following well-known graph from a recent study:

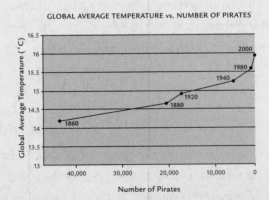

GLOBAL AVERAGE TEMPERATURE vs. NUMBER OF PIRATES

As you can see, there is a statistically significant inverse relationship between Pirates and global temperature. But of course not all correlations are causal. For example, take a look at this seeming correlation regarding ID proponents:

It would appear that the people behind ID have a lower intelligence quotient than the general population—and a significantly lower IQ than scientists, who overwhelmingly reject the idea of Intelligent Design.[14]

14. Henderson, 2005.

I, for one, tend to believe this to be merely a strange coincidence, and that ID believers are not necessarily as retarded as the data would suggest. It is entirely likely that the Flying Spaghetti Monster put this coincidence in place in order to confuse us further as to our true origins. We may never know.

SCATTER PLOT FOR BELIEF IN ID

x = ID Supporters   • = Scientists

FSM vs. Other Religions

A conversation about Intelligent Design proponents, no matter how brief and specious, inevitably leads us to a discussion about God and religion. It is important to state up front that the Church of the Flying Spaghetti Monster is a peaceful religion—probably the most peaceful of them all. But can we prove that? In order to explore our proposition, let us look at religion and violence throughout history, particularly with regard to war and death.

Christianity appears to be the Rambo of religions, with the Crusades, the Inquisition, various bloody rebellions, the Conquistadors . . . the list seems nearly endless. Suffice it to say that when Jesus Christ stated, in his bewitching and Yoda-like manner, "But those enemies, which would not that I should reign over them, bring hither, and slay them before me,"[15] people took him pretty literally. The Jews[16] and the Muslims haven't done so well for themselves either, and are still duking it out. We even find Buddhists fighting in China. So, glossing over the evidence, we find that religion can be quite scary and violent. On the other hand, there's absolutely no evidence of any deaths from FSMism, which seems to imply that it has the lowest death rate. And if that is true, then this is strong evidence that FSMism is the most peaceful religion.

Now take a look at how much criticism of Christianity, Islam, Judaism, and the other religions there is. People can't seem to decide on the simple things, like which holy book to follow, let alone whether any of it is true. There are arguments between friends and countries, tens of thousands of books on the various religions, all poking holes, jibbering about which god to worship (Hinduism), jabbering about which ancient prophet's cousin to support (Islam). It's a mess. And yet we find that exactly, count them, zero books have been written to poke holes in the theory of the Flying Spaghetti Monster. There isn't even any academic criticism, only academic support—and academics love to argue about everything. All this we take as evidence that FSMism is probably true.

Finally, we find that the religions tend to put a lot of stock in "dogma," which is a way of saying they are correct beyond all doubt. Even the most devout of the Pastafarians will scratch their heads and nervously readjust their eye patches at this idea. Dogma implies an absolute belief in something, and in order for people to have an absolute belief in *anything*, they'd basically have to be fucking omniscient.[17] We have a different approach: FSM believers reject dogma. Which is not to say that we don't believe we're right. Obviously, we do. We simply re-

15. Luke 19:27.
16. Who managed to knock off Jesus, if you believe some people.

17. Which would be cool, but would probably also make you a little uncomfortable around other people.

serve the right to change our beliefs based on new evidence or greater understanding of old evidence. Our rejection of dogma is so strong that we leave open the possibility that there is no Flying Spaghetti Monster at all. So, in a sense, you could say that we're extremely open-minded—we could change our minds someday. All we ask is proof of His nonexistence.

The fossil record is loaded with evidence of His existence. You just have to know where to look.

An Alternate Vision

A Note from
Peter J. Snodgrass, Ph.D.,
and the Imam Perez Jaffari

RE: UD in a Not-So-Intelligent World

When confronted with the grim realities of war, famine, pestilence, diarrhea, and Celine Dion, it is not entirely surprising that one might be led to consider that our Creator, while all-powerful, might not have proven Himself to be completely infallible.

While there can be no doubt that the source of creation was indeed the Flying Spaghetti Monster (FSM), and that He did leave mysterious and ambiguous clues to throw us off track,[1] we submit that the FSM was careless, cruel, drunk, or even high when he first laid down the template for life as we know it. How else to explain the extinction of 99.9 percent of all plant and animal species ever to exist on earth? How else to explain the release of not one, but two Deuce Bigalow films?

Without question, we are members of a small and limited minority of scientists and religious leaders who deign to question the Creator's wisdom in allowing for life-threatening volcanoes, tsunamis, hurricanes, twisters, and plastic surgery gone bad, but as the evidence accumulates, we can only posit one undeniable theory:

The FSM, our Creator, isn't very bright.

Undoubtedly, this statement represents a subtle paradigm shift, especially when juxtaposed against the common perception of a

1. For instance, making Evolution seem plausible.

benevolent, all-knowing Creator, but innumerable examples of questionable judgment do exist. Something is certainly rotten in Denmark when Ben Affleck is allowed to bed both J.Lo and that hottie from *Alias*, while Matt Damon is forced to date his own assistant. We cry foul!

So we hereby state our belief that the universe is a result of "UNINTELLIGENT DESIGN" (UD).

Casting social science aside, we can turn to the physical sciences to support our claims.[2] Why doesn't the Benevolent and Noodly Master get to work and start eradicating mass poverty, cancer, global warming, and nuclear proliferation? Is He too busy trying to rekindle the low-carb diet craze?

While this treatise might not appear to meet the normal requirements of an academic paper, let it be said that such was not even our intention. This is a work composed by a scientist *and* a religious leader. If science and religion are to live side by side in mutual non-judgment, there needs to be a new model for dialogue, one that takes into account the interests of *both* sides. Religious people don't really "do" numbers. Scientists can't get dates and don't have a clue what real people think. By collecting and presenting a different kind of data, we aim to appeal to "Bible thumpers" and "brainiacs" alike. Just getting those epithets out on the table can make a difference.

In fact, we feel better already. Too many resources are being wasted in trying to prove intelligence in all we see around us. Wouldn't it be better just to throw in the towel, call a spade a spade, and admit that our Creator is a dumbass?

2. The Patel Paradox: Dr. S. Patel, Ph.D., notes that the Hubble constant reveals a universe that is expanding at a rate both measurable and significant. In spite of that fact, he still can't find a parking space.

Examples of Unintelligent Design

1. **THE DODO.** Portuguese sailors, who marveled at this bird's trusting and docile nature, gave it the name dodo, meaning "simpleton." Unfortunately, the dodo was unable to compete in a rapidly changing environment,[3] and the bird soon went the way of the Portuguese sailor.

2. **THE PASSENGER PIGEON.** Once the most populous bird in North America, the passenger pigeon's demise can be traced back to the early 1900s and McDonald's highly popular but short-lived "McPidgin Sandwich."

3. **THE IRISH ELK.** Neither exclusively Irish nor an elk (it was really a large deer), the male of this species attracted mates based on the size of its antlers: the larger the antlers, the more attractive the male. As the selective pressures for a "nice rack" increased, the head of the male grew so overburdened that the males began to fall easy prey to the large predators[4] that were moving into northern Europe at the time. All the less impressive males just drank themselves to death.

4. **THE LLAMA.** The typical llama is unable to produce milk or eggs, and many people can't even spell its name.

5. **THE APPENDIX.** Might once have had value but is now completely useless.[5] No one really knows why it remains, although some have been found to hold gold coins.

6. **RELIGIOUS WARFARE.** Someone has described religious warfare as "killing people over who has the best invisible friend." We tend to agree.

7. **DISCO.** Scientists are still split on this dance craze, but the FSM doesn't like it, so it goes on the list.

8. **THE MACARENA.** True fact: invented by a guy named Retardo.

9. **JAR JAR BINKS.** Hesa just stupid.

10. **THE DUCK-BILLED PLATYPUS.** Q. What creator combines a duck with a muskrat? A. Not an intelligent one.

3. Possibly caused by an early aboriginal dot.com boom.

4. Saber-toothed tigers, Germans, etc.

5. This includes its presence in book form.

Aboriginal children killed the dodo.

FSM vs. ID, an Unlikely Alliance

The Controversy: Peer Review

PEOPLE ARE PLAYING POLITICS with science.

Supporters of Intelligent Design, or ID, have been targeting education officials and public policy makers in a blatant attempt to have their views taught to our nation's students as "science." Because 99 percent of the scientific community supports the theory of Evolution, ostensibly rejecting ID in the process, we find ID proponents arguing that their beliefs should be *taken directly to the public*—thus letting disorientated high school biology students decide the issue once and for all.[1]

1. See chart below.

This contrasts significantly with conventional scientific methods, where researchers are required to submit their work for review by fellow scientists in their particular field—a process known as "peer review." Such a system serves to weed out unacceptable theories, thus keeping science pure and permanently safe from controversy. But ask yourself this question: While "peer review" sounds like a good idea, is turning to one's peers for their opinions not the wrong way to go? Is it not the same as a woman asking her boyfriend, "Do I look fat in this blouse/dress/parka?" Regardless of the item of clothing being worn,

NATIONWIDE POLL OF A CROSS SECTION OF "AVERAGE" HIGH SCHOOL BIOLOGY STUDENTS	
What is your opinion of Evolution?	
"Cool"	7 percent
"Awesome"	8 percent
"Stupid"	14 percent
"Is that a new band?"	8 percent
Didn't have a #2 pencil	62 percent
Asleep	1 percent

the answer is a resounding "no, you look great" in 99.99 percent of all test cases.[2] As a consequence, we argue that the highly secretive "peer review" system is unfairly hardwired to reinforce the limited viewpoints of scientists and their close friends.[3]

If the scientists had their way, we wouldn't be discussing ID at all today. In fact, you'd have to go all the way back to the Salem witch trials before you'd find such close-mindedness and raw hatred for other people's views.[4] But brave school board members—nearly all of whom have no scientific background and, in some cases, very little education—have declared the current system to be unfair. With the courage of witches, they have dared to step forward and redefine science, and we of the Church of the Flying Spaghetti Monster have decided to stand by them.

And so we throw our hats into the ring:

We have uncovered remarkable evidence suggesting that the Flying Spaghetti Monster is behind the theory of Intelligent Design, deftly manipulating the debate with His Noodly Appendage.

If Not Him, Then Who?

If we take the Intelligent Design proponents at their word—that ID is not religious in nature but simply a scientific alternative to Evolution—then the religious background of the proponents of ID should closely mirror that of the general public. However, when we look at the data, we do not see the expected result. Instead, we find that 95 percent of leading ID proponents are evangelical Christians, or ECs. Given that evangelical Christians do not even attain such high densities in the South, we estimate that there is a .001 percent chance of this nearly 1:1 ratio of IDs to ECs occurring naturally. Again, accepting the claim that ID is a science and not a religion, the only other inference we can draw is a supernatural one.

ID proponents are extremely careful to state their arguments in secular language, avoiding calls by many to declare the identity of the designer. When one looks at ID it is clear that a creator must be present;

2. The lone .01 percent of yeses coming from either idiots, assholes, or male high school students who may or may not be using the colloquialism "phat."

3. The belief that scientists don't have any friends is a misapprehension. They like to hang out with other scientists, and sometimes computer programmers, and talk about themselves.

4. See *The Crucible* (20th-Century Fox, 1996), in which Winona Ryder accuses several girls of "practicin' Satan's magic in Ye Olde Shop" in an effort to mask her own shoplifting.

however, the ID proponents are tight-lipped as to who that creator might be. If it's a Christian God, why not mention it? You'd think this would be important enough to at least be stated somewhere. This leads us to determine that the designer is *not* a Christian God. But if that's the case, then who is behind the controversy?

Clearly, the FSM is behind it. Who else could influence such a uniformly religious group of people to subscribe to the non-Christian, nonreligious theory of ID? The FSM is notorious for just this type of mischievous intervention, and thus it can only be concluded that the FSM is behind the ID movement, which makes sense when you think about it.

Irrefutable Proof

Some of the greatest thinkers of all time have dedicated their lives to proving the existence of God. Thomas Aquinas gave it his best shot, and his writings have been confusing college freshmen ever since. Kurt Gödel used a proof that appears to have employed hieroglyphics; unfortunately, no one can read hieroglyphics anymore, so we don't know if he was successful. Suffice it to say, no one has managed to prove the existence of God, and as a result, ID doesn't seem to be provable either.

And that's what we find in the record. Since ID offers no hypotheses of its own, which is a requirement of science, it cannot be considered a scientific theory unless we can prove the existence of God.[5] So it turns out that the scientific community has good reason to be skeptical of the theory of Intelligent Design. But ID proponents rightfully claim error or conspiracy on the part of scientists. And here's the hitch: There is no conspiracy . . . but there is a consPiracy.

5. Just saying that a creator made the world, when you haven't proven that there is a creator, doesn't count.

Ax 1. ∙ ∀x{[φ(x) → ψ(x)] ∧ P(φ)} → P(Ψ)
Ax 2. P(¬φ) ↔ ¬P(φ)
Th 1. P(φ) → ◊ ∃x [φ(x)]
Df 1. G(x) ↔ ∀φ[P(φ) → φ(x)]
Ax 3. P(G)
Th 2. ◊ ∃x G(x)
Df 2. φ ess x ↔ φ(x) ∧ ∀ψ{ψ(x) → ∙ ∀x[φ(x) → ψ(x)]}
Ax 4 P(φ) → ∙ P(φ)
Th 3. G(x) → G ess x
Df 3. E(x) ↔ ∀φ{φ ess x → ∙ ∃x φ(x)}
Ax 5. P(E)
Th 4. ∙ ∃x G(x)

Gödel's proof of God: completely unreadable.

The truth is that the FSM is hidden all around us. And He's left clues like Italian-style bread crumbs to show us the path to His Eternal Noodliness. He's in our language—every time someone tells you to use your "noodle" they're unknowingly directing you to turn to Him for guidance. And whenever someone talks about a "consPiracy," they're just invoking the mischievous nature of Him and His Chosen People, the Pirates.

But language alone isn't undeniable proof for those skeptical scientists.[6] We need cold, hard facts. To begin, we will look at how the Evolutionary scientists try to pick apart the work of ID scientists, men like Michael J. Behe, who argues in his seminal and frequently incoherent tome, *Darwin's Black Box: The Biochemical Challenge to Evolution*, the concept of irreducible complexity. Somewhere toward the beginning, Behe makes the following damning statement: "By *irreducibly complex* I mean a single system composed of several well-matched, interacting parts that contribute to the basic function, wherein the removal of any one of the parts causes the system to effectively cease functioning."[7] He then goes on to talk about "Evolutionary mechanisms" and "the emergence of some complex biochemical cellular systems" and other things that, let's face it, sound like mumbo jumbo to laymen and high school biology students.[8] But the point is that this is well-thought-out science, nearly irrefutable proof that Behe can talk like a scientist. While the Evolutionists respond with computer simulations demonstrating that it is possible for irreducible complexity to evolve naturally, I would note that it is also possible for me to use my computer to lead an entire army of samurai warriors against the greatest generals of their day. Call it a wash.

Both sides have their points to make, but the Church of the Flying Spaghetti Monster proposes a simple answer that is more likely, and immensely more plausible, which is that the Flying Spaghetti Monster is altering our scientific data in an effort to mislead us. It's not the scientists' fault, for how could they know? The FSM is invisible and passes through normal matter with ease.

While our theory may sound a lot like Intelligent Design, there are

6. Arguments based on language are useless against scientists, since none of them have read a real book in years.

7. Whew! Talk about complexity (*Darwin's Black Box: The Biochemical Challenge to Evolution* by Michael J. Behe, Free Press, 1996, p. 39).

8. Same thing.

important differences between ID and FSMism, the most important being that they are wrong and we are right. But we do have some things in common, and I think it's important that these are addressed.

Like ID, we use a slightly nonconventional scientific method, whereby we first define our conclusion and then gather evidence to support it. Not only does this allow for a more congruous and fluid study, but it has to be said that research is much easier when you've already chosen your conclusion. In this regard, the ID proponents should be congratulated for their ingenuity. Where before scientists were forced to grapple with unknowns for months, or even years, they will now be able to simply choose a convenient conclusion and find evidence to support it. And to be completely honest, even though we share this new scientific methodology, the ID people must get the credit for developing it first.

Perhaps one day soon the ID community, too, will be touched by His Noodly Appendage and join forces with the Pastafarians. The time has never been better. Indeed, we live in exciting times, when our nonconventional supernatural theories are finally being given equal credence as the natural, or "unbiased, evidence-supported" theories. We should all feel fortunate to be living in such open-minded times.

And now, ladies and gentlemen, we have some proving to do!

Communion Test

Abstract

WHILE SUPERNATURAL EXPLANATIONS provide surprisingly irrefutable evidence that the Flying Spaghetti Monster is (1) present in the universe, and (2) actively using His Noodly Appendage to spread goodness and affordable nutrition to the true believers, it is important to provide quantifiable evidence in support of our claims. As such, we have devised a scientific test as proof of His existence. This test is both repeatable and easily verifiable by a third party, and the Church of the FSM encourages all doubters to use the following *experimental evidence* to prove to themselves what we already know to be true.

Background

It has been suggested that the communion served by the Church of the Flying Spaghetti Monster will lead to better and more long-lasting nutritional benefits than, say, the Christian communion. Through deductive reasoning, this can be taken to provide evidence of His Noodliness.

Method

As support for this thesis, we selected two subjects[1] of average height, weight, and intelligence. We then placed them on a seventy-two-hour fast in order to reduce outside factors. After seventy-two hours, one subject was given the Christian communion, consisting of a paper-thin wafer. The other subject was given the FSM communion, consisting of a large portion of spaghetti and meatballs.

1. People.

Results

Both subjects had their vitals recorded before and after communion. Upon completion of the test, the Christian was found to be listless, with decreased heart rate, body temperature, and brain function. The Pastafarian recorded increased heart rate, body temperature, and brain function, commenting that he felt "full," which we interpreted to mean *whole.*[2]

2. That is, the FSM test subject was showing signs of His presence.

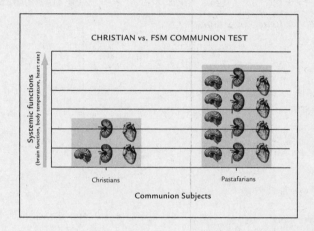

3. Although this is a supernaturally based study, it is important to highlight that nosy scientists want to see proof that their "peers" will support. Therefore, we agree to jump through a couple of hoops, if that's what it's going to take to make them see His Noodliness.

Addendum

4. Probably due to the fact that communion wafers are basically made out of cardboard.

Some may say that 1,200 calories of spaghetti versus 2 calories of wafer do not make a fair and valid experiment, and they may have a point.[3] We have sought to keep the experiment as close to a realistic communion setting as possible, but in the interest of science, we've devised an additional experiment, whereby each subject receives the same total number of calories. Our findings were that the Christian became violently ill upon consuming 2,500 calories in wafers (or 1,250 wafers)[4] while the Pastafarian continued to show increased vitals, thus illustrating His Noodly Presence.

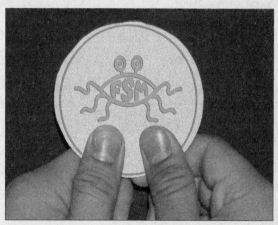

Sacrilicious

Unified Spaghetti Theory

The more we learn about the world around us, the more we see that life and the universe were created in His image. From interconnected forces on the grandest of scales, down to matter's tiniest bits, we see His Noodliness in everything. To illustrate this, we have devised the following simple recipe.

Life

INGREDIENTS

  Boiling water
  Elementary particles made from "string"
  Salt

Life evolved from hot, boiling springs.

Before the Flying Spaghetti Monster made life, He had to first make the elementary particles that would eventually compose all matter as we know it. This was a very complicated process, but we have developed a much simpler method, one that you can try at home. First, take a piece of subatomic "string," which naturally is just an incredibly small strand of wet spaghetti, so tiny that it cannot be seen by even the most powerful of microscopes. Next, give the string a unique vibration. Now repeat, giving each new string a different vibration so as to create more unique particles. Congratulations! You have created particles of matter. Be sure to collect the particles into a secure vessel for later use.

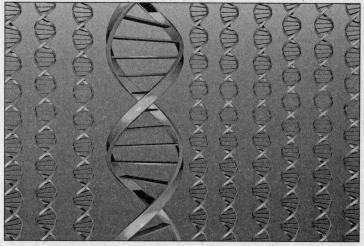

Now we are ready to make life. In order to re-create the steaming "primordial broth" that originally spawned life, you must first bring your water to a heavy boil. Salt liberally. Now add your elementary particles and wait about an hour.[1] When you begin to see small spiral components forming—they will resemble fusilli when they're ready—that means you're almost there. Remember not to drain the water! Now apply intense overhead heat for about an hour.[2]

Continue boiling and applying intense overhead heat. Eventually, you will begin to see small "organisms" appearing in your broth. Give yourself a pat on the back: You've created life!

Artist rendition of what a very small piece of spaghetti might look like.

1. Cooking time may vary.
2. Or possibly several million years.

A careful review of the evidence shows clearly that life was generated from the simplest piece of pasta,[3] and that all life has since radiated to more or less resemble His image. But the Spaghedeity didn't stop there. In fact, science tells us that the universe itself is composed of nothing more than an enormous matrix of strings, vibrating to their own Noodly music, forming a single, unified, coherent framework of invisible spaghetti. In short, it's all one eternal bowl of pasta.

3. Pagan scientists have misidentified it as "strings."

More attentive readers will note that we've failed to address the image of *man*. While other religions make the claim that humans were created in God's image—and they are *nearly* correct in this assumption—they are guilty of using reverse logic to reach this conclusion. What they don't discern is that we were created in His *ideal* image: that of the Pirate. Since then we've only come to resemble other people's gods.

DNA, which is the building block of life, bears a striking resemblance to fusilli pasta.

It is important that we return to the ways of the Pirate before it's too late. In fact, recent science suggests that our departure from the Pirate's way has led us toward a previously unforeseen end. As our brains and bodies grow in size, and as machines[4] replace the need for physical strength and agility, we may find ourselves the victims of an ironic twist of Creation. If current trends persist, the day may come when people of the future actually *do* resemble His image. This illustration, which was created by a scientist, may help.

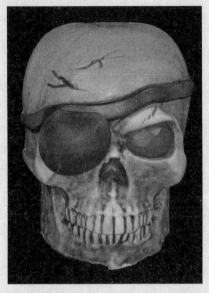

Convert or die!

4. For example, motorized wheelchairs.

With this evidence in mind, we suggest that you get yourself an eye patch and become a Pastafarian before it's too late.

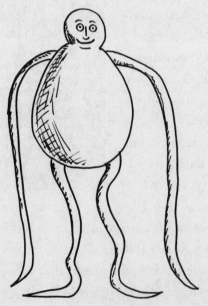

The future of mankind?

Early Life: In His Image

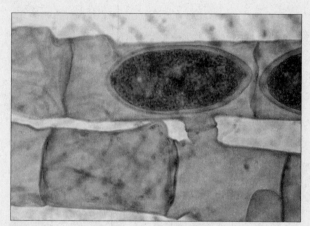

Spirogyra.

Proteus flagella.

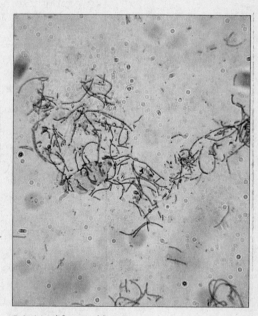

Primitive life resembles His Noodliness.

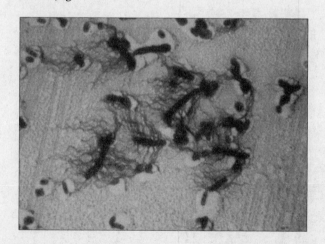

More Evidence

THE MAJORITY OF PROOFS of His existence appear to come from scientists, and scientists appear, in large part, to come from colleges and universities. Therefore, we thought it would prove enlightening to look more closely at these institutes of higher learning and try to find some evidence of His Noodly Appendage at work.

We came up with some interesting results.

1. See every college graduation speech through time.

Life on Campus

It is well known that college students are our best hope for the future.[1] These intrepid individuals are willing to pay thousands of dollars of their parents' money just to read books, so it goes without saying that learning is very important to them. But what exactly are they learning?

If you examine the research on this subject you will see that, while many students do in fact spend time reading books of knowledge, they also spend equal or greater amounts of time drinking beer. You may ask what beer has to do with learning, and many doubters will argue that there's no link whatsoever, but we have uncovered some surprising evidence for the benefits of beer consumption. Beer acts as an important nutritional supplement to the college student, but that's not really important. Beer[2] is also the official beverage of Pirates, who are His Chosen People. With that in mind, we ask you: Could the Flying Spaghetti Monster be behind this? Is he trying to turn college students back into Pirates?

2. Also known as "grog."

Furthermore, it's an accepted fact that there are an uncanny amount of Ramen noodles and dried pastas on college campuses, which provide cheap nutrition for students, thus allowing them to afford more beer. This points yet another finger at the Flying Spaghetti Monster's influence. Clearly, He is at work in our institutions of higher learning, and this can only bode well for the country's future.

Money

College costs money—a lot. Yet education in itself is not of much value. For example, we can look to the general public's almost complete disregard for anything that educated people have to say about global warming, shrinking oil reserves, pollution, or the

Dollar bills, y'all.

threat of nuclear annihilation. But if this is true, why does something as worthless as a college diploma cost so much money? To understand this question, we examined the unique and often bizarre relationship between college and money, and our research led us to an interesting finding.

It appears that a college education has been given an artificially high price tag in order to leave students with little money left over for the basic requirements of living. Burdened by poverty, students are induced to drink cheap beer and eat pasta—in short, they are forced to act like Pirates and Pastafarians—and we can only conclude that this is some part of His greater plan to spread FSMism. If the students truly are our future, so, it would appear, is Pastafarianism.

Food for the soul.

Poorly evolved? . . . Or just lazy?

Kiwi Birds: Flightless?

EVOLUTIONISTS CONTEND that flightless birds—for example, the kiwi bird of New Zealand—never developed the ability to fly. The old argument goes that, having no natural predators in their area, there was never a reason to evolve the ability.

While I'll agree that I've never seen a kiwi bird fly, I disagree with the statement that they can't fly. How do we know? Couldn't it just be that they choose not to? You'll never see me running, but there's a good chance I could.

Kiwi birds, besides being completely spherical, are well known to be one of nature's laziest animals. Consider the speed with which they are going extinct—it is almost as if they are trying to get eaten. I contend, then, that they *can* fly, but simply lack the proper motivation. So, to settle the debate once and for all, I've devised an experiment that any Evolutionist may carry out in an attempt to prove me wrong.

Dump Truck Over Cliff

You will need as large a sample size as possible for this experiment, as some kiwis are bound to be lazier than others. Twenty to thirty is probably sufficient, but it's better to err on the side of too many if you have a sufficient supply. Load the birds into the back of a truck and proceed to the highest cliff available—we want to give them as much motivation to fly as possible. After backing the truck to the edge of the cliff, incline the bed and dump the birds over the edge.

I suspect that the birds, seeing their fate rushing toward them at terminal velocity,[1] will flap their "useless" wings and fly to safety.

Until such time as this experiment is carried out—or one similar to it—I will consider my hypothesis to be correct.

1. Throwing them out of an airplane might work better. In addition, perhaps a kiwi bird sitting in a blender would be motivated to fly out before the switch is thrown.

EXPLAINING PASTAFARIANISM

Man cannot live by bread alone.

—MOSES, DEUTERONOMY 13:7

A Condensed History of the World

Five Thousand Years Ago: The Beginning

THE FLYING SPAGHETTI MONSTER created the universe and a bunch of planets, including Earth. No one except Himself was around to see it, but we suspect it was rather dull. The initial creation, obviously, must have been spectacular, but He then spent the next ten to one hundred years painstakingly preparing the universe to appear older than it actually is. Photons were placed individually, en route to earth, ostensibly emitted millions of years ago from stars across the galaxy. In reality, we know that each photon was divinely placed and red-shifted[1] appropriately to make the universe appear to be billions of years old. We are still finding His camouflage methods at work today; each time scientists discover apparent evidence of a billions-of-years-old universe, we can be assured that this is just more elaborate preparation He put in place.

Earth was created in approximately 0.062831853 seconds and was similarly disguised to appear much older. We can be certain that the FSM spent even more time preparing the earth, because, being all-knowing, He was well aware that soon enough there would be nosy people poking around everywhere. Known as "scientists," these nosy people have a sick need—probably sexually motivated[2]—to figure out how things work, and so it was even more important that our apparent reality be well designed to hide the truth.

Our Noodly Creator then placed fossils, hidden under the earth's surface, knowing that they would later be found—thus, seemingly proving that these creatures existed some time ago. Dinosaur bones, for example, were placed so well and in such numbers that it's widely believed dinosaurs roamed the earth millions of years ago. Interestingly, dinosaurs did exist, but not millions of years ago, because, of course, how could they have existed before the earth was even here? In reality they lived *with* us, alongside—and occasionally on top of—humans around three thousand years ago.

1. The universe appears to be expanding, much like cooked pasta, as illustrated by observed light from distant galaxies shifting toward the Marinara Spectrum. Some scientists cite this as support for His preference for red sauce, but they are most likely idiots.

2. As evidence of sexual motivation on the part of scientists, let's choose an occupation at random, say gynecology. These so-called professionals spend their entire lives looking at female sex organs—or poontang, as it's known in academic circles. Look a little deeper into the fold, and you will find that nearly 99 percent of all gynecologists have a scientific background. To illustrate just how significant that is, pick another group at random—say, myself. I'm not a scientist, and I hardly ever see female sex organs. I find it hard to believe this is just a coincidence. I'm not saying all scientists are perverts, but I think it's safe to say that nearly all of them are.

You may wonder why we find no bones from dinosaurs from this era, and rightly so. But keep in mind that dinosaurs don't actually have bones—the whole *dinosaurs had bones* thing is all an elaborate hoax planned for His own divine amusement. Real dinosaurs, as any enlightened paleontologist—or *bone doctor*, as they prefer to be called—will tell you, were able to stand erect by engorging selected muscles with blood, making the once flaccid limb rigid. By alternating which muscles were engorged in the correct sequence, a very effective locomotion and rudimentary skeletal structure was achieved. Perverted readers may recognize that this mechanism is similar to what happens in the male penis. Dinosaurs were, in essence, not much more than a massive collection of penises (penii) under a thick skin. While very few accurate descriptions of these creatures have existed into present times, we can be pleased to learn that awareness of them has propagated generationally in our culture. Most men don't even realize that when they exaggerate the size of their penis—referring to it as "monstrous" or "dinosaurlike"—they are helping to keep alive the hidden truth of the strange and horny beasts we know as dinosaurs.

Some time later, as society progressed, the attention of mankind moved away from dinosaurs—by now they had been conquered and placed under the control of men for work and play—and instead man turned to philosophical thought. The question of our origins came up, and it was decided, based on the apparent natural evidence, that all creatures had evolved from a common ancestor over time some millions of years ago.

Twenty-five Hundred Years Ago: The Golden Age of Pirates

What happened next is still a mystery. Mankind up until this time had been successfully duped by the FSM, wrongly believing that natural explanations could explain our origins. One would think that the FSM Himself would be pleased by this, as He had gone to so much trouble disguising His creation work. But for whatever reason, He felt the need to expose the truth to us. This was the date, some twenty-five hundred years ago, that He first revealed His Noodly Appendage to us, showing us the way. From this point on, those who accepted His message knew that we were to live a certain way—on the water in great wooden ships, loaded with grog, swag, and, hopefully, wenches. This was His will, and so it was done.

Unfortunately, many of the details from this era are lost to us, possibly because many ships sank, due to overloading. Swag is very heavy, and these, the first Pastafarians, showed less than 100 percent perfect judgment, having drunk too much grog. What we do know, though, is that this was the Golden Age of the Pirate lifestyle. Millions, possibly hundreds, of Pirate ships roamed the world's oceans and maybe lakes, searching for a good time, spreading joy and maybe VD to whomever they came into contact with.

What we're told of Pirates in history books today is blatantly wrong. Thieves and outcasts they were not—these were His Chosen People, the ones who listened and followed His divine plan, whatever it was. The commonly propagated myth that Pirates were thieves can be traced, un-surprisingly, to the Christian theologists of the Middle Ages. It's just another example of the discrimination and misinformation that we've had to contend with over the years, and another reason Pastafarians have been so secretive about their beliefs.

Regardless of the lies told about them, the first Pastafarians were peace-loving explorers and spreaders of goodwill, not bloodthirsty criminal Pirates. In fact, they were well known to distribute candy to passing children, thus establishing what is now known as Halloween.

Of course it was not all good times. Not everyone was a believer, and some rejected His Word and felt the need to go out on the ocean in their own (probably lame) ships and pick fights with the Pastafarians. Most notable was Noah, of biblical fame, who slapped together a monstrous barge made of wood and whatever else was around—probably dirt, who knows? Noah, well known for his love[3] of animals, always had plenty around. So when he found himself with a lack of building materials, he

3. Perverted coveting.

decided to use hundreds of defenseless animals as ballast—mainly the slowest, dumbest, and most dense that he could come across.

It's not known exactly what occurred during this time of Noah and the Pirates, but enough historical texts have survived through the years to get a rough picture of the events that transpired. Noah, alone except for his animals/ballast, propelled by jealousy and maybe a group of talking seals, set forth in search of Pastafarians. Unfortunately for Noah, he found one of the most bad-ass Pirate ships around, and started talking way too much smack. The Pastafarians, being above all peaceful, and maybe drunk, ignored his verbal abuse. It was only when Noah, ever the dick, physically attacked the Pastafarian ship by hurling from his bow the pointiest of animals[4] that the Pastafarians took notice. We are told that the largest, scariest of the Pastafarians swam, or maybe just jumped, from ship to ship—they were that powerful—and confronted Noah.

Immediately seeing the error of his ways, Noah offered some turtles or something as a way of apologizing. The Pastafarians, probably having plenty of their own turtles,[5] said no deal, and proceeded to intimidate the bejesus out of Noah. We don't know exactly what was said, but it's clear that Noah wet himself to such an extent that even Christians associate him with "the Great Flood."[6] Needless to say, he never mistreated animals again—not even chickens, who are pretty much asking for it.[7]

1700 to Today: Of Pasta and Pirates

For centuries after that, no one messed with the Pirates, and the natural order of things was kept in balance. Although swag and grog sent many a ship to the bottom of the sea, losing important historical documentation in the process, the Pirates lived a life of peace and merriment, spreading His Word as far as places like Belgium.

They continued to celebrate Halloween and, during the last two months of every year, took time off from sailing the seas to relax and spend time with their families during their most holiest time of Holi-

4. Possibly these were porcupines. Also, some scholars believe that Noah might have hurled stab-rabbits, a since-extinct species of rabbit possessing weaponlike points all over its body. Despite their love of sex, the stab-rabbits ultimately went extinct because they could not bring themselves to go through with copulation, the pain being too great—much like modern-day men who are married to fatties.

5. Giant ones, for riding.

6. Although they have wisely developed another description of events.

7. There are no mentions of Pirates or grog, and only a few of wenches in the Christian Bible.

day.[8] But there were dark storms on the horizon, and the Pirates did not know what evil awaited them.

Convinced of the inherent evil of Pirates, Hari Krishnas, who are descended from Ninjas, banded together at various seaports[9] and declared a holy war against the Pirates. By tens of thousands, maybe even dozens, they boarded steel-plated kayaks and paddled out in search of Pirates, whom they intended to annihilate from the four corners of the earth. You might think that the FSM would have noticed the Hari Krishnas and protected His Chosen People, but He mistook the Krishnas for just another musical band of seagoing beggars, or maybe fishermen singing their shanties, and He let them pass unharmed. As the first Krishnas arrived at a Pirate ship on Halloween, the Pirates mistook them for overly dedicated trick-or-treaters. What followed next was mass slaughter as the Pirates tried to pass out treats while the Krishnas beat and sliced them to death with their double-bladed kayak paddles. Sadly, this pattern was repeated several times that day. The next year was even worse.

Eventually, the Pirates retreated to hidden coves where they could keep a lookout for the bloodthirsty Krishna bastards. Was there something in the Krishnas' singing that blinded the Pirates to their evil? We may never know. And while mainstream education tells us that Pirates were hunted down because they were thieves, killers, etc., this is largely a misinformation campaign propagated by the Krishnas and many of the other religions that banded together to begin their systematic assault on the Pirates' worship of the FSM.

Hunted nearly to extinction, the Pirates were indeed quite pissed off for several centuries, and the textbooks reveal every detail of the looting and pillaging but are suspiciously quiet about the fact that Pirates were well known for passing out candy to children.[10] The sad truth is that the other religions were jealous of the Pirates and their happy lifestyles—it's that simple. Thankfully for the Pirates, the attacks eventually slowed down and then nearly stopped altogether as the other religions inevitably turned against one another. Which is where we find ourselves today.

8. Today, portions of this period are known as various holidays—Christmas, Chanukah, Kwanza, and others—except at Wal-Mart, where it is still considered Holiday, as in "Happy Holiday, and Welcome to Wal-Mart."

9. And later at airports.

10. If you ever read a Pirate textbook, you'd think they were Jesus.

While it is becoming common knowledge that declining Pirate numbers are a direct result of religious persecution, what is not yet known is what happened to the remaining Pirates and where they are located.

Sadly, many Pirates simply hid their treasures, gave away their giant turtles, and retired, moving to places like Ireland[11] and, ironically, India.[12] Others hid out in the Straits of Malaysia, while some formed well-known sports franchises. What is little known about our mystical forerunners is that in addition to hiding treasure, Pirates sought to conceal their religious texts. In fact, the treasure was included largely to ensure that others would go out and look for these documents in the future, during more tolerant times. On this count, the Pirates were wildly successful, as there are still treasure hunters searching for ancient Pirate loot. Unfortunately, many of our original texts have been lost, as their importance was overlooked, being mistaken for recipes in some cases.

11. Most Celtic artwork resembles the FSM (see illustration), which leads us to believe that many Pirates simply became druids. Also, there is a striking similarity between midgets and leprechauns.

12. Possibly believing that all the Hari Krishnas had moved to California.

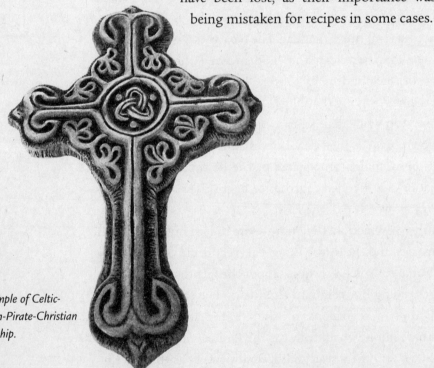

A fine example of Celtic-Pastafarian-Pirate-Christian craftsmanship.

Key Moments in FSM History

hey say that a picture is worth a thousand words, and since we're well into the book now, and tired, we thought it would be helpful to provide some key moments in Pastafarianism—Photoshop-style!

This early cave painting suggests that the FSM might have tried to interfere with aboriginal hunters in an effort to get them to eat more pasta. Ultimately, He succeeded, only to see the aborigines establish a world-wide chain of mediocre steakhouses.

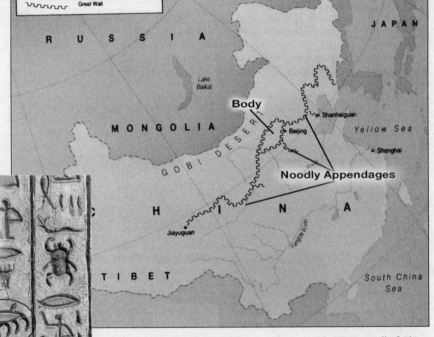

THE GREAT WALL OF CHINA · 204 BC

National boundary
Great Wall

The Great Wall of China, one of the few man-made objects that can be seen from the heavens, is suspected to be a tribute to the FSM.

The pharaohs sought protection from the FSM in the afterlife. In spite of their wealth, it appears that they're still waiting.

Originally misidentified as cracks, this partial pedimental sculpture of the FSM reveals that Western civilization was founded on a deep reverence for Pastafarianism.

Somehow Michelangelo snuck this one past the pope. Since then it has gone on to become one of the most commonly downloaded pieces of art ever produced.

TOUCHED BY HIS NOODLY APPENDAGE

Intimidated by the FSM's great intellect, the Founding Fathers decided to include a clear separation between church and state. They wouldn't even let Him sign their declaration and had His image painted over in the final portrait.

Sometimes the FSM has to interfere in the misguided affairs of man. Here He encourages Douglas MacArthur to accept the Japanese surrender after World War II. (In the background, several pirates can be seen standing at attention.)

When Ben Franklin described electricity as "a Noodly power cast down to earth," he was more correct than people realized.

Einstein secretly consults the FSM, who reiterates that He indeed does not play dice with the universe.

You didn't think NASA got us there all on their own, did you?

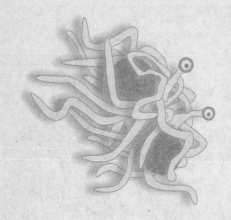

Bobby Answers the Big Questions

Q: What sort of pasta is the Flying Spaghetti Monster made of? Wheat? Semolina?

A: There's some debate about this—Western culture contending He is wheat-based, while in the East they believe He's made of rice or buckwheat. We don't know the truth, and maybe we're not meant to.

Q: Why do modern-day Pirates, sports teams called "Pirates," and Pirate costumes not affect global weather, given that there is a statistically significant link between Pirate numbers and global temperature?

A: Calling oneself a Pirate, or dressing up as one, does not make one a true Pirate; it takes much more. In what way are modern-day "Pirates," with their speedboats and machine guns, similar to the fun-loving adventurous buccaneers from history? How can sports teams, with their obsession over rules and regulations, claim to embody the mischievous spirit of the Pirate?

Dressing up as a Pirate comes closer, and we can sometimes see an effect on weather. Halloween Pirates, for example, are at least trying to emulate true Pirate behavior, sometimes with important details such as wenches and grog. We can see solid evidence that they are indeed making a difference on weather patterns; the several months following Halloween are always colder than the several preceding it—just as the Pirates-temperature causal relationship predicts.

Talk Like a Pirate Day (www.talklikeapirate.com) is another good example of how acting like a Pirate can influence the weather. Every September 19, millions, if not thousands, of people communicate in Pirate-speak, a subtle nod to their Creator, and a conscientious effort to curb global warming. And with great success. Since its creation several years ago, the temperature on September 19 each year has been colder than on the day I picked scientifically at random—July 10—without exception. Just a coincidence? Unlikely.

Q: How do you reconcile the glaring inconsistencies and contradictions in the FSM religion?

A: First, all of these seeming flaws were carefully put in place, by Him, to test His followers' faith. Second, a certain amount of inconsistency is necessary for a religion to become widespread—for example, Christianity, Islam, and so on.

Q: If the FSM is benevolent, why do bad things happen to good people?

A: They may have angered Him, or it could be that He is too busy, or indifferent for whatever reason, to get involved. He works in mysterious ways that we are not always able to understand.

Q: Does He hear my prayers?

A: Yes, but that is not to say they will necessarily be answered. To increase your odds, it's recommended that you wear Pirate regalia or at least an eye patch.

Q: Are the other religions wrong?

A: No, they're just misguided. We accept converts from other religions with open arms.

Q: What about atheists and the followers of other religions—heathens—will these people go to Hell?

A: No, but they may not be allowed into the best areas of FSM Heaven. The safest thing to do is to convert now. Think of it this way: If you convert to Pastafarianism, and the FSM turns out not to exist, nothing is lost. On the other hand, if you don't convert, and the FSM does exist, then you have just been royally screwed.

Q: If there's a Beer Volcano and a Stripper Factory in Heaven, what's FSM Hell like?

A: We're not entirely certain, but we imagine it's similar to FSM Heaven, only the beer is stale and the strippers have venereal diseases. Not unlike Las Vegas.

Q: Are there male strippers in FSM Heaven for women?

A: Probably, but they are invisible to the non-homo guys.

Q: Your "religion" offends my (probably Christian) beliefs.

A: That's not a question.

Q: Your "religion" offends my beliefs. What should I do about feeling mocked?

A: Our alternative beliefs are in no way mocking your beliefs more than yours mock ours. FSM believers are peaceful, open-minded, well educated, and reject dogma outright. We've never started a war and have never killed others for their opposing beliefs. Compare our record to yours.

Q: Where does the FSM exist?

A: We're not sure exactly, because He's invisible most of the time and rarely makes His presence known. Prayers don't seem to reach Him until well after they're prayed. This leads us to believe there is some sort of time dilation effect. Plus, so many prayers are offered to Him that even He wouldn't have the time to hear them all without a time dilation effect. For this reason, we suspect He spends a great deal of time orbiting a black hole.

Q: Does the FSM have a sense of humor?

A: We can see the FSM's sense of humor by looking at the way He deals with other religions. Consider how often evangelical Christians, those who ostensibly promote peace, are aligned with pro-war groups. Clearly, this is the work of the FSM, bringing together opposites. If there was no divine influence, the conflict of interest would be obvious to both groups; that they can't see it smacks of Noodly interference.

WWAPD?

I N THESE TRYING TIMES, where the world keeps shrinking and the trappings of modern society—cell phones, computers, PDAs, video games, taxes, war, pornography, and microwavable dinners—are crowding in around us, oftentimes a person feels lost. Where do we fit in this modern world? What's our purpose on earth?

Many are mired in eternal confusion, swept against the shoals of too many choices. Maybe you feel this way right now.

If so, don't lose your faith. Instead, close your eyes and think back to a simpler time when the choices were fewer, when life passed as long days under the benevolent sun, and a man knew where he stood. Even if it was on a peg leg.

If life has got you down, simply ask yourself: *What would a Pirate do?*

Asking this question will no doubt lead you along a path that starts at a local inn, where the first answer awaits you . . .

1. A PIRATE WOULD DRINK SOME GROG.

If grog isn't the bread of life, it's certainly what you need to keep that bread from catching in your gullet. Grog opens the mind and frees the soul. It also frees the inhibitions, so be mindful in your search that you don't obtain grog goggles. Too much grog can make for questionable bunkmates, and if you're wearing an eye patch you're already a couple of cards behind in the game.

Once the mind has been appropriately lubricated, you may find that it wanders. This is good, for a wandering mind is a searching mind. And yet, if the mind strays too far, you may find yourself asking the wrong questions or even turning forgetful. Which leads you to . . .

2. A PIRATE WOULD OBTAIN A PARROT.

Parrots are renowned across the seas for repeating (or "parroting") the words of humans. When a Pirate can't recall what he's just said, he can always just wait a second or two for the parrot to repeat his words (for example, "Aaaak! Me hook is caught in me bonnie's blouse"). A good parrot is essential to a happy and prosperous life of plunder, but parrots are about as scarce as Pirates these days. In a pinch you can substitute a computer, PDA, or even a diary to do your parroting for ye.

But computers, PDAs, diaries, and parrots are no substitute for true bonhomie. And drinking alone, even with a parrot perched on your shoulder, is not the Pirate way. This brings us to step three:

3. FIND YE A BAND OF MARAUDERS.

All the greats had a merry band of marauders to assist them—toothless, unshaven, and smelly. Seek for yourself a group of similar ilk. They will lift you up when you are down. And when you are whipped up into a bloodlust, you will find that they ground you. Blackbeard speaks of a time when he was at his most vulnerable—he looked back on the beach to see only one set of foot and peg leg prints. It was then that his first mate, "Ol' Longshanks," had carried *him* along the shore. Words to live by.

Once you have found your grog, your parrot, and your band of marauders, you are ready to act like a true Pirate. And what does a Pirate want most? He wants a Pirate ship . . .

4. IF YOU CAN'T STEAL ONE, BUILD YAR SHIP.

A Pirate just isn't a Pirate if he doesn't own a seaworthy vessel. You may have an eye patch, you may even have a parrot and a peg leg, but the true goal of any Pirate worth his weight in doubloons is to gain a means of travelin' the Seven Seas. A ship gives you true meaning. It provides transport and opens the world to ye. Without one, you're just a guy in a funny outfit.

So now ye have the trappings of a real Pirate. What are ye going to do with 'em?

5. FIND THEE A WENCH!

Or if you're a wench, find thee a Pirate![1] Wenches and Pirates go together like spaghetti and spaghetti sauce.[2] Now hit the seas and take what's comin' to ye!!!

1. Female Pirates should find themselves a stout male Pirate.
2. So do same-sex Pirates, who are perfectly acceptable in Pirate culture.

The journey is a long one, and the voyage can sometimes be monotonous—long hours spent with the same merry band, consuming the same grog and gruel for months on end, bunking with the same wench. There's only one way to avoid Pirate malaise.

6. When in doubt, plunder!!

The only way to avoid inaction is to take action. Examine yer charts and locate a sleepy fishing village.

Then plunder it!

Find a town inhabited by wealthy noblemen.

And plunder them!

These days it's too easy to sit back and find excuses. If you want to see what's out there, go see it. Then plunder, plunder, plunder.

With these basic Pirate principles, you should be able to live out your days in happiness and prosperity. Follow them at all times, remembering their importance most when you're lost and in the doldrums. And if by chance you find that you *still* can't put wind into your sails, remember this last point . . .

7. Arrrgh!!!

To accept the Pirate life is to accept the eternal Arrrgh!!! Without it, you're just another landlubber.

The Holy Noodle

The First Day: Light

WHEN THE FSM SAID, "Let there be light," and there was light. And the FSM adjusted his willowy eyestalks and saw that the light was good; and the FSM divided the light from the darkness. He called the light Day, and the darkness He called Night or "Prime Time." So the evening and the morning were the first day.

The Second Day: The Firmament

The FSM was tired of flying and He couldn't tread water for very long, so he said, "Let there be firmament in the midst of the waters, and let the firmament form coves to one day provide safe harbor for Pirates—no, wait, firmament is a stupid word; let it be called *land*, since 'firmament-ho!' sounds even stupider than just plain firmament—and let this land divide the waters from the waters. And let there be a volcano to spew forth beer, which seems like a benevolent idea." And the volcano spewed forth beer and He tasted it and declared it to be quite good. So the evening and the morning were the second day.

The Third Day: Land and Vegetation

When the FSM awoke, his thoughts were muddled and He didn't know where He was. Slightly hungover, and somewhere out in the Indian Ocean, the FSM found himself a little confused about what He'd created the day before; and so, self-conscious about the previous night's misbehavior, He started barking Godlike orders in an attempt to reestablish His powerfulness, and then the FSM decided to organize. He said, "Let the water under the heavens be gathered together in one place, and let the dry land appear" (having forgotten about Day Two's firmament command), and He called the dry land Earth (having only yesterday come up with the term *Land*), and the gathering together of the waters He called Seas. And the FSM dried His Noodly Appendages under the hot Light, and He saw that it was good but that there was a little problem. For now He had an earth full of Land *and* Firmament, which wouldn't do. So he lifted Day Two's firmament up to the heavens and renamed it Heaven. The land from Day Three He left where it was. Heaven seemed like the sweeter pad, and the FSM decided He'd live there and commute to the earth. Then the FSM said, "Let the earth bring forth grass, semolina, rice, and whatever else can be turned into food that resembles my Noodly Appendages," and He saw that this was an original idea, which was certainly good. That night He drank a little less from the Beer Volcano, which was relocated to Heaven along with the rest of the firmament. So the evening and the morning were the third day.

The Fourth Day: the Sun, the Moon, the Stars

At this point, the FSM was a little sore from overexertion. It was difficult for Him to find a comfortable resting position during the night, which was darker than squid-ink pasta would eventually be. So He said, "Let there be lights in the heavens, and let there be two lights: the greater light to rule the day, and the lesser to rule the night." And since He had big plans for the next day, He turned in early. So the evening and the morning were the fourth day.

The Fifth Day: The Big Bang

The fifth day was going to be huge, so the FSM rose early. Then He said, "Let the waters abound, let the skies fill with birds, let the earth bring forth creatures, each according to its kind. Then let them canoodle and be fruitful." And He saw that it was good, and He was feeling pretty proud of Himself, so He hit the Beer Volcano hard that afternoon.

Later that evening He rolled out of bed and landed hard on the firmament, and this, fair reader, was the true Big Bang. He had a funny feeling and realized in His drunken stupor that He had not only built a factory in Heaven that turned out scantily clad women in transparent high heels, but He'd also created a midget on earth, whom He called Man. And He said, "Wow. Even I might have overreached my Noodly Appendage on this one," and not even sure what day it was anymore, He decided to take an extended break from the whole creation gig, and He gave a quick blessing and declared, "From here on out, every Friday is a holiday."

The Olive Garden of Eden

That midget, however, was goddamn noisy. The FSM couldn't deal with all the complaining down on earth, so the Lord FSM commanded the midget, saying, "Here's an idea . . . why don't you collect the semolina, rice, and what-have-you, and make pasta in my image. That's what it's there for. And fill your mouth with it and be quiet and peaceful. But be careful with the olive tree, for the olive itself is good, but the pit inside is rock hard and you could choke on it or break a tooth, so you should consider it as *evil*; if you choke on it you shall surely die, which would mean I wasted a hell of a lot of time on you, although I'm already having second thoughts."

Man wasn't excited about eating pasta seven nights a week, so the FSM broke down and brought him all the animals, and Man renamed each as a food group. Cattle he called "beef." Pigs he called "pork," "ham," or "bacon." Strangely, Man stuck with "chicken" for chicken. Perhaps Man was tired at this point and had lost his sense of creativity.

The FSM suggested that Man take a nap, so he did. When he awoke, the FSM said, "Man, have I got a surprise for you. Check this out. *Woman!*"

The midget stared blankly for a moment, then said, "Can I keep her?" And the FSM said, "From now on a man shall leave his father and mother and be joined to his wife, and they shall become one flesh," and then the FSM thought to Himself, *This should be interesting.*

"I owe you one," said the midget-man.

Before long, Man broke his damned tooth on that olive pit, and the FSM said, "What did I give you ears for if not to listen to me?" And Man said, "I have ears?" And he eventually located them on the sides of his head, but not before discovering a small Noodly Appendage between his legs, which he noticed was infinitely smaller than even the shortest of the FSM's appendages, and he realized that his woman appeared to be thinking the same thing, so the midget-man said, "Hand me one of those fig leaves, will you?"

Later the woman suggested that Man didn't need such a big fig leaf, and she hinted that there might certainly be another Man somewhere on earth, maybe Eden had a gardener somewhere, and the midget-man looked her up and down and said, "One word, honey. *Cellulite*."

Then the eyes of both of them were opened, and they knew that they were naked; and they sewed fig leaves together and made themselves coverings. And they heard the sound of the FSM floating around the Olive Garden and they hid and said, "What are you doing here?" Then the FSM said, "Where are you?" Man said, "I heard you floating around over there, and I was afraid because I was naked; and I hid myself."

And the FSM said, "That's fine, but can you tell me where you hid those delicious breadsticks? I haven't eaten since the Creation."

"We ate them all," the midget-man lied. "There aren't any more breadsticks left."

The Flood

Then the FSM saw that the wickedness of Man was great on earth, and that every thought of the little midget was ruled by his stomach.

Then the FSM said, "Fine, I'll just cook for myself," and He produced a great Colander of Goodness and He did collect water in an enormous pot, which He heated; and He did drop in a heaping portion of pasta and slowly simmer the sauce for so long that the original humans weren't even around anymore when He was finally ready to eat. And He poured the spaghetti and water into the Colander of Goodness, careful to make sure that the water went down the drain of His sink. And as He was eating, He vacantly considered where the drain did empty, and the FSM said, "Uh oh."

Luckily, Noah and Noah's sons, Ham, Cheese, and Omel, and Noah's wife and the three wives of his sons with them, had been working on "Big Noah's Floating Menagerie," which was to be housed in a giant ark of Noah's design. On that day all the fountains of the great deep were broken up, and the drains of the heavens were opened. And the rain was on the earth forty days and forty nights, and the ark did float but it did stink.

After several battles with Pirates, the ark did finally rest on Mount Ararat, and when the waters receded it was a long walk home for Noah and his family. And no one could locate the unicorn pair, but they did discover Noah's son Ham in a back chamber of the ark, picking his teeth with an oversized toothpick that remarkably resembled a horn.

The Tower of Scrapple

Like Noah, his sons were real entrepreneurs, and they did spread out— Ham went to the southern nations and started the Hamites; Cheese went to the central nations and started the Cheese-Its; and Omel journeyed northward to start the Omelets. There they did establish family diners to supply the locals with foodstuffs.

Ham, who was a bit of a troublemaker and always looking to squeeze out a few extra sheckels, determined to develop a foodstuff that could be produced from the leftover pig snouts and sawdust that did normally just get thrown in the garbage at the diner. He ground up this waste and did call it "scrapple." And he did enlist the help of Nimrod to help market the scrapple. Needless to say, it wasn't a fast seller, and the scrapple did pile up out behind the diner, sitting under the sun until it formed a sort of wretched tower.

Since they couldn't sell it for food, Nimrod suggested they call it the Tower of Scrapple and charge a fancy sum for passersby to come behold its majesty. "A fool is born every minute," he said to Ham, and Ham agreed.

Shortly thereafter, the FSM started noticing a bad smell around the firmament. He floated down and declared, "That thing, and I mean this quite literally, stinks to high heaven. What do you think you're doing?" Thinking fast on his feet, Nimrod said, "We built it as a tribute to your greatness." But the FSM wasn't buying it. "I thought I told you to be fruitful and fill the earth," He said to Nimrod. "And not with *flies*, with people." Nimrod didn't have a response to that, so the FSM told him, "Just tear it down."

Since the Tower of Scrapple wasn't the tourist draw he'd hoped for, Nimrod bowed to the FSM's wishes. Unfortunately, he inhaled too many rancid scrapple fumes in the process, and he was rendered a babbling idiot.

Mosey

And the diners did prosper, and the population feasted and grew in number until there were so many short-order cooks that Phil the night manager did fear a revolt to his authority.

And he ordered that no more short-order cooks be hired, but one young boy named Mosey, who couldn't sit still and was always running his mouth, did talk his way into a job by claiming to be able to cook "the best papyrus on rye this side of the Euphrates."

Mosey did indeed cook a mean papyrus, and he was an artist with the deep fryer, but he did grow tired of the long hours and mistreatment, and one day he walked into his manager's office, threw down his apron, and said, "I'm tired of the nine to five. I'm quitting to become a Pirate."

That got the FSM's attention, and he kept careful track of Mosey. In fact, years later, the FSM, who had grown tired of Phil's mistreatment of the short-order cooks and was getting to be in a generally bad mood, found Mosey camping out in the desert, drawing up plans for a massive Pirate Ship, and the FSM spoke to Mosey through a burnt roasted marshmallow and commanded Mosey to go back and lead all the short-order cooks out from under Phil's control. The FSM bade Mosey to hire the cooks and start a restaurant of his own, preferably one that specialized in foods more to His liking. "Maybe call it the Olive Garden. You could manage the kitchen staff," said the FSM. But when Mosey returned to the diner, Phil refused to release the short-order cooks' last paycheck if they followed Mosey.

Now the FSM was really angry with Phil, and He punished him with the following plagues:

1. A rain of spaghetti sauce
2. A hail of linguini
3. Repetitively playing Kid Abyssinia's rap hit "I'm the Makkeda Daddy" inside Phil's head

Phil relented, and the FSM commanded the short-order cooks to celebrate the yearly "Pastover," where the angel hair pasta of death passes over all the houses that have a smear of sauce on the doorpost.

Now the FSM spoke to Mosey, saying, "This month shall be the beginning of your new restaurant franchise; it shall be the first month of the rest of your life. Speak to all the short-order cooks, saying 'Begin your sauce on the tenth day of this month. Every man shall prepare a sauce, stirring it occasionally. If you don't have enough people to eat it, go over to your in-laws' house.

"'Now you shall cook the sauce until the fourteenth day of the same month. And you shall take some of the sauce and smear it on your doorpost. Then you shall pour the remainder of the sauce over a heaping bowl of the pasta of your choosing, and you shall eat all of it.

"'With a belt at your waist, a patch over your eye, and a cutlass in your hand, you shall eat the pasta. For you are no longer short-order cooks, but the sauce on your door will mark you as Pirates!'"

Though Phil had reluctantly agreed to release the last paychecks, as soon as Mosey led the short-order cooks out of the diner, he changed his mind. Phil chased after them, all the way to a giant red puddle of spaghetti sauce that had been left over from the first plague. The FSM parted the Red Puddle for Mosey, but He didn't notice that Phil was hot on his heels. Unfortunately, Phil was swallowed up by the puddle and rolled into a giant meatball.

Mosey became "Pirate Mosey," and later dried pasta fell from the skies like manna, which is Hebrew for "monster."

The Eight "I'd Really Rather You Didn'ts"

Pirate Mosey really wanted that Pirate ship, and putting all labor issues aside he declared his band to now be Pirates, and he led the Pirates up to the top of Mount Salsa, where he thought there might be a good chance of finding the Pirate ship he'd been searching for all these years. But they didn't find the ship, and the people didn't know how to act like Pirates—after all, they were really just a bunch of short-order cooks—and the FSM came down and declared that they'd better clean up their act, because *real* Pirates belonged on the open seas, not on a mountain. And Pirate Mosey was embarrassed and wouldn't come down from the mountain, even though the rest of his band took the FSM's advice and went down into the town at the bottom of Mount Salsa to wait for their captain. Finally, the FSM got completely fed up, and He visited Mosey on the mountaintop and told him where to find the sea, and, after admitting that it had been a long haul since Creation and that maybe He'd even rethink some of His decisions if He had it to do all over again, He gave Pirate Mosey some advice, which came in the form of ten stone tablets. These tablets Mosey called "Commandments" (since he had a healthy sense of drama)—although the short-order cooks grew confused and misnamed them the "Condiments"—but because of the phrasing, the FSM refers to them as the "I'd Really Rather You Didn'ts." Unfortunately, Mosey dropped two of them on the way down the mountain, which partly accounts for Pastafarians' flimsy moral standards, but the rest can be read as follows:

The Eight "I'd Really Rather You Didn'ts"

1. I'd Really Rather You Didn't Act Like A Sanctimonious, Holier-Than-Thou Ass When Describing My Noodly Goodness. If Some People Don't Believe In Me, That's Okay. Really, I'm Not That Vain. Besides, This Isn't About Them So Don't Change The Subject.

2. I'd Really Rather You Didn't Use My Existence As A Means To Oppress, Subjugate, Punish, Eviscerate, And/Or, You Know, Be Mean To Others. I Don't Require Sacrifices And Purity Is For Drinking Water, Not People.

3. I'd Really Rather You Didn't Judge People For The Way They Look, Or How They Dress, Or The Way They Talk, Or, Well, Just Play Nice, Okay? Oh, And Get This In Your Thick Heads: Woman = Person. Man = Person. Samey-Samey. One Is Not Better Than The Other, Unless We're Talking About Fashion And I'm Sorry, But I Gave That To Women And Some Guys Who Know The Difference Between Teal And Fuchsia.

4. I'd Really Rather You Didn't Indulge In Conduct That Offends Yourself, Or Your Willing, Consenting Partner Of Legal Age AND Mental Maturity. As For Anyone Who Might Object, I Think The Expression Is Go F*** Yourself, Unless They Find That Offensive In Which Case They Can Turn Off The TV For Once And Go For A Walk For A Change.

5. I'd Really Rather You Didn't Challenge The Bigoted, Misogynist, Hateful Ideas Of Others On An Empty Stomach. Eat, Then Go After The B******.

6. I'd Really Rather You Didn't Build Multimillion-Dollar Churches/Temples/Mosques/Shrines To My Noodly Goodness When The Money Could Be Better Spent (Take Your Pick):
   A. Ending Poverty
   B. Curing Diseases
   C. Living In Peace, Loving With Passion, And Lowering The Cost Of Cable

I Might Be A Complex-Carbohydrate Omniscient Being, But I Enjoy The Simple Things In Life. I Ought To Know. I AM The Creator.

7. I'd Really Rather You Didn't Go Around Telling People I Talk To You. You're Not That Interesting. Get Over Yourself. And I Told You To Love Your Fellow Man, Can't You Take A Hint?

8. I'd Really Rather You Didn't Do Unto Others As You Would Have Them Do Unto You If You Are Into, Um, Stuff That Uses A Lot Of Leather/Lubricant/Las Vegas. If The Other Person Is Into It, However (Pursuant To #4), Then Have At It, Take Pictures, And For The Love Of Mike, Wear A CONDOM! Honestly, It's A Piece Of Rubber. If I Didn't Want It To Feel Good When You Did IT I Would Have Added Spikes, Or Something.

RAmen.

A History of Heretics

Everyone knows that Pirates are badasses. But history is also full of non-Pastafarians who have dared to rock the boat, challenging the limits of religious and scientific dogma alike. With this in mind, we offer this rundown of heretics through time. Their poor lives illustrate just how hard a world without FSMism can be.

Aristotle:
New Age Philosopher

Aristotle was born in northern Greece a really long time ago. He was the son of a wealthy and influential doctor, and studied under Plato,[1] who was also the son of a wealthy and influential doctor. Thus began the Greek tradition—a key forebear to contemporary Western thought—which holds that the wealthy and influential shall grow even more wealthy and influential, while the poor and fluential grow poorer and increasingly lose their fluent.[2]

Because Aristotle dared to disagree with the teachings of Plato, he was not appointed head of the Academy when Plato died. Angered by this snub, Aristotle took a tutoring job with a young Alexander the Great, whom he encouraged to follow his dream of raping, pillaging, and eventually taking over the world.

After that, Aristotle retired to his writings. It is said that Aristotle wrote over 150 treatises. Although that is an awful lot of treatises, they can be summarized as follows: Everything in our world is composed of *potential* (matter) and of *reality* (form). Like an uncarved block of marble, we have the potential to "sculpt" our lives and make them into whatever reality we wish. Today, this line of thought is referred to as

1. Today Plato is nearly forgotten. His beliefs include the notion that people who govern should be intelligent, rational, self-controlled, and in love with wisdom, an idea that has long been discredited.
2. Loose translation from the original Greek.

"freaky New Age shit," and contemporary scholars agree that, if Aristotle were alive today, he would definitely be a fixture on *Oprah*.

Aristotle has been a fan favorite of all the great thinkers throughout time. Not only was he a great philosopher, but he also developed a systematic classification of animals, which made him quite the Renaissance man, and it should be noted that his teachings experienced a real renaissance during the Renaissance. But there were dark clouds ahead for his Renaissance supporters . . . for although he talked a lot about God, he also declared that the universe was eternal, a belief that caused a lot of trouble about a thousand years after he died, when the Catholic Church finally started paying attention to all the Aristotle hype.

Leonardo Da Vinci:
Architect, Musician, Anatomist, #1 New York Times
Bestselling Author, Inventor, Vegan, Engineer,
Homosexual, Sculptor, Painter,
and Minor-League Stickball Prodigy

Known as the original Renaissance Man, Leonardo Da Vinci came from humble origins. His father was a notary and his mother was a local peasant woman. Leonardo was raised on the hard streets of Florence where he grew up quickly—learning to draw, paint, sculpt, and invent before normal kids his age had ever even *seen* a gun. He was also a closeted homosexual.[3]

Da Vinci began keeping journals early in life. He wrote them in code, but his cowriter, Dan Brown, later translated much of what was inside. Through Da Vinci's journals, as well as surviving records kept by Florence's Officers of the Night, an antisodomy agency of the time,[4] we have learned that Da Vinci enjoyed the company of adolescent boys and that he "liked 'em young." He also became a vegan,[5] having determined that milk-producing udders are homologous to a woman's breasts, which of course he despised. But enough about his sexual preferences.

Throughout Da Vinci's life, he managed to invent everything that's

3. Da Vinci invented the closet.

4. This was a real group; we are not shitting you.

5. Essentially a hard-core vegetarian, who doesn't even eat milk or eggs, and can't stop talking about it.

ever been used in a war. These include the helicopter, the hang glider, the tank, the machine gun, the cluster bomb, the robot, and the submarine. Later he went on to invent the single-span bridge, the video game Halo, and the gate that swings both ways.

The Renaissance humanists saw no distinction between science and the arts, and so Da Vinci didn't limit his brilliant imagination to just inventing things.[6] He also painted such famous masterpieces as the *Adoration of the Magi*, the *Mona Lisa*, and *The Last Supper*. He studied anatomy, designed festivals, sculpted, and wrote music. He even arranged it so that his shit didn't stink. In short, he was awesome.

(We will not cover Da Vinci's problems with the Catholic Church, since everybody has already read *The Da Vinci Code*.)[7]

6. By contrast, today's scientists are only interested in science, *Star Wars,* and video games.

7. By Dan Brown (Doubleday, 2003).

Giordano Bruno:
Deserved What He Got

Originally born with the name Filippo in 1548, Giordano Bruno took his new name in 1565 when he became a Dominican friar at the Monastery of Saint Domenico near Naples. Eventually he was ordained a priest, which is slightly ironic considering what the Church eventually did to him. But more on that later.

Disliked by all who encountered him, Bruno became an avid reader of books. He read Plato, Copernicus, Thomas Aquinas, Averroës, Duns Scotus, Marsilio Ficino, Nicholas of Cusa, Nick Hornby, and Isaac Asimov. It is a well-known fact that those who read books often develop some funny ideas, and history has shown this to be especially true of people from the olden days. Bruno became particularly influenced by his reading of Copernicus and Plato—so much so that he couldn't stop talking about them. In 1576 the Inquisition put Bruno on their Ten Most Wanted list.

He escaped to Geneva, but this wasn't the last time the Inquisition would come calling. For a short period, Bruno joined the Calvinists, but he was unwilling to abide by their strict "no smiling" policy. In 1579 he traveled to Toulouse, France, where, for a while, he enjoyed the protection of powerful French patrons. It was during this period that he completed the majority of his writing, including *De l'infinito universo e mondi,* in which he argued that the stars were the same as our sun, that the universe was infinite, and that all universes were inhabited by intelligent beings, establishing Bruno as the first ever sci-fi geek.

While still in France, Bruno gained fame for his prodigious memory. Although his ability to retain information might have been a direct result of his intensive reading habits, he really should have put down the books at this point and slipped into dispassionate ennui like the rest of the French. Instead, Bruno decided to go to England.

In 1583 he sought a position at Oxford, but the people there judged him to be a know-it-all and Bruno was turned away. After petitioning to teach at a few other English schools, he came to learn the harsh reality of the saying "You only have one chance to make a good first impression."

For the next couple of years, it is believed that Bruno spied against Catholics in England. Posing as a Catholic priest, he purportedly took confessions from Catholics, then reported those confessions to English spymasters who saw to it that the Catholics were put to death under the persecutory laws of the time. Even if Bruno wasn't a heretic, he most surely had proved himself to be a major asshole by this point—and well-deserving of a good burning.

In 1585 Bruno returned to Paris. Within a year he had pissed off the Parisians, and so he moved to Germany, where his reputation hadn't preceded him. By 1588 he was on his way to Prague, and it was growing clear that Bruno was running out of countries.

Faced with the option of fleeing to Siberia[8] or going back to Italy, Bruno stupidly accepted a brief teaching position at Padua in 1591. Unfortunately for him,[9] the professorship he sought there went to Galileo Galilei. So he journeyed to Venice, where he pissed off one last person, who then denounced him to the Inquisition.

Bruno was arrested on May 22, 1592. It took six years before he stood trial in Rome, and when the inquisitor, Cardinal Robert Bellarmine, asked him if he still stood by his beliefs, Bruno is believed to have replied: "Does the pope wear a funny hat?"

8. By this point, Siberia was the only place that hadn't heard of him.

9. Though probably fortunate for everyone else.

And so, on February 17, 1600, a nail was driven through his tongue, Bruno was tied to a stake, and he was burned as a heretic.

If only he'd kept his mouth shut.

A tough lesson, for sure.

Charles Darwin:
Evolution's "Creepy Little Cook"

In June 1837, more than twenty years before Charles Darwin published his famous, if highly flawed, treatise on Natural Selection entitled On the Origin of Species, *the young biologist self-published a lesser-known work, one that turned out to be his first stab at reconciling his beliefs in science and religion. That book was* On the Origin of Spaghetti Sauce.

The Early Years

Probably mildly retarded, Darwin grew up in Shrewsbury, England, the fifth of six children. He was the son of Robert Darwin, a well-to-do doctor, and Susannah Darwin, who was rumored to be a virtual magician in the kitchen. Throughout Darwin's life, this family dichotomy would tear at the very fabric of his being, as pressure to excel in the natural sciences collided with his more homey desire to transmogrify the English culinary experience, a mission at which he ultimately failed.

Darwin entered Edinburgh University in 1825 and was immediately astonished to discover that the university did not offer courses in the culinary arts. Tricked by his father into studying medicine, the dejected young Darwin resorted to cooking sumptuous dinners for himself in his boardinghouse. In his second year he joined several student naturalist societies, and for a short time he was free to explore the shores of the Firth of Forth, collecting crustaceans for various culinary wonders, like linguini with clam sauce and penne with striped zebra mussels. Little did his fellow students realize that this "creepy little cook"[10] would one day use these experiences as a springboard for one of the greatest revolutions in Western contemporary thought.

While still at Edinburgh, Darwin produced his first scientific paper. Presented to the Plinian Society, it explained that the black spores found in oyster shells were the eggs of the common skate leech. Darwin shrewdly concluded that these spores were left by the Flying Spaghetti Monster as a sign that even the lowliest of God's creatures could band together for a common cause.[11] He was soundly laughed out of the society's chambers, and shortly thereafter his father arranged to have him transfer from Edinburgh to Cambridge.

Once he got to Cambridge, Darwin's father threatened to remove young Charles's colander and other kitchen utensils if he did not bear down and fully commit himself to his studies as a physician. But the young son was adamant that he would follow his dream of culinary excellence. When he finally threatened his father with the prospect of abandoning the family and moving to France, the two Darwins arranged a secretive meeting in Paris's Saint-Sulpice Church,[12] where it was determined that the young Darwin would pursue studies in theology. This seemed a sensible compromise, as clergymen were well paid and as most English naturalists were clergymen. Charles is widely believed to have told his father at the time, "If I cannot be allowed to explore the wonders of God's cookery, then let me at least explore the wonders of His creation."

Charles Darwin applied himself at Cambridge but was a C minus student at best. In the summer after that first year at Cambridge he was embarrassed by his poor showing and sought any means possible to avoid going home during the break. He read a bunch of pamphlets and ultimately decided to take a Mediterranean cooking cruise, where he was promised the opportunity to explore and sample the various foods of Greece and southern Italy. But the voyage was ill-fated. Darwin suffered from food poisoning and sea sickness, and ultimately he went

10. As quoted in Phineas P. Cornflower's autobiography *Aye, I Knew Darwin's Sauces.*

11. In this case, oysters served as "babysitters" for skate leech eggs so that adult skate leeches would be free to pursue their insatiable urge to drain the lifeblood from skates.

12. *The Da Vinci Code,* Doubleday Books, 2003

home early. The only record of these sad days exists in a poorly penned and unpublished journal that he titled *The Voyage of the Meatball*.

The Voyage of the Beagle

The Voyage of the Meatball nearly destroyed Darwin. He limped through his last year of studies and, following graduation, did what any man armed with a Cambridge degree would do: He took a five-year vacation to the Galápagos Islands. Suffering from nervous exhaustion—and having lost all faith in humanity—Darwin was now determined to befriend as many of the world's animals as possible.

It was aboard the HMS *Beagle* that life began to turn around for him. In a freak gale off the coast of Tierra del Fuego, all of Darwin's cookbooks were washed overboard; bored and suffering from severe skin rashes, young Charles picked up a book that would set his life on a new course. That book was Charles Lyell's *Principles of Geology*, which posited that geological features are the outcome of gradual processes that take place over eons of time. Something clicked in Darwin's head, and in that moment of clarity he realized that a slow-cooked sauce would be exponentially more delicious than one that was merely heated from a can, something that had never before occurred to an Englishman. From this realization, he gleaned some other ideas related to Evolution, but he was really most excited about the sauce revelation. Within days, the *Beagle*'s cook was thrown overboard, and Charles Darwin took over the ship's mess.

There were mussels galore in South America,[13] and Darwin thrived. On October 2, 1836, he returned to England as a minor celebrity, having discovered fossils, finches, tortoises, mockingbirds, and modern cooking. His book *The Voyage of the Beagle*[14] was a hit, and he was invited to dinner parties throughout London, where he cooked and talked throughout many a night. Some of the proceeds from the *Beagle* book went toward self-publishing *On the Origin of Spaghetti Sauce*, in which Darwin put forth his theory of slow-cooked sauce and perfectly boiled

13. Sadly, many of them were fossilized.

14. Having a similar structure and tone as *The Voyage of the Meatball*.

noodles as a divine representation of the Flying Spaghetti Monster. Sadly, the book never took off.

Still, Darwin had his day job, which consisted of little more than jotting down everything he noticed. To that effect, and prompted by the fascinating structural similarities between earthworms and various forms of pasta, he began studying worms.[15] It is quite possible that this is the point where Charles Darwin finally descended into full-blown dementia. We will, however, never know the full truth, because Thomas Huxley, who had developed an unhealthy fascination for the fullness and length of Darwin's beard, took it upon himself to follow Darwin around in an attempt to defend his mindless ramblings about worms.

It was Huxley who convinced Darwin to stop arguing that humans were descended from worms—or "in His[16] image," as Darwin was often quoted as saying. Huxley convinced his friend to claim that the lines of descent passed instead from *monkeys*, which he pointed out actually *had* appendages and bore an uncanny resemblance to certain people, including Darwin, who became known as "Monkey Man."

Once Darwin made the intellectual jump from worms to monkeys, his theory really took off. He was invited to many official scientific meetings, where he was lauded by geniuses, savants, and even scientists and philosophers. To this day, no one really knows why.

15. Darwin loved worms—describing them on several occasions as "noodly" and "so without appendages as to be appendages themselves."

16. "His" refers to the Flying Spaghetti Monster, of course.

The End of His Life

In 1842, embarrassed by his fame, and mortally disappointed by his inability to realize his life's ambition of being a professional chef, Darwin retreated to Down House in the London Borough of Bromley to "write that damn egghead book," as he put it.

He published *On the Origin of Species* in 1859, which was mostly about worms and the animals he'd befriended while vacationing in the Galápagos, rendering it completely unreadable. Later he wrote *The Dessert of Man*, which Huxley changed to *The Descent of Man* without Darwin noticing.

Destitute and nearly forgotten, Charles Darwin died in Downe, Kent, England, on April 19, 1882. His beard was eight feet long at the time. [17]

17. *Guinness Book of World Records.*

John Scopes: The ACLU's Little Monkey

On May 25, 1925, John T. Scopes was charged with violating Tennessee's Butler Act, which prohibited the teaching of Evolution in Tennessee schools.[18] Scopes was eventually found guilty and given the choice of paying a $100 fine or being pummeled with rotten fish and burned at the stake. After much reflection, he chose to pay the fine.

18. See Stanley Kramer's stunning five-part documentary *Inherit the Wind*.

Scopes later admitted to reporter William K. Hutchinson that he had never actually taught his class about Evolution, choosing instead to skip the lesson altogether. In fact, his most famous quote is the Clintonesque "I didn't violate the law." But if Scopes didn't teach Evolution, how did this trial come about?

As usual, the ACLU was behind it.

It turns out that lawyers from the ACLU had offered to finance a test case challenging the constitutionality of the Butler Act. Scopes became their unwilling monkey, and the lawyers started pouring into Tennessee by the hundreds. The defense team included Clarence Darrow, Dudley Field Malone, John Neal, Arthur Garfield Hays, and Frank McElwee, among others. The prosecution included Tom Stewart, Herbert Hicks, Wallace Haggard, Ben and J. Gordon McKenzie, William Jennings Bryan,[19] and William Jennings Bryan Jr. Before the trial even started, the ACLU had met its objective of employing as many lawyers as possible, and the real tragedy of the Scopes Monkey Trial is not that it helped to promote the teaching of Evolution, but that it was an early model for our highly litigious society.

19. Who was still trying to make up for his embarrassing "Cross of Gold" speech, in which he argued that Pirates had used their treasure to forge the first Christian cross.

After the trial, Scopes attended the University of Chicago, where he earned a master's in geology. He then went on to work for the oil industry, where in 1932 he met a young oil executive named Dick Cheney, who disclosed to Scopes that he would "one day take over the world."

Dolly the Sheep: "She Was a Whore"

Code-named "6LL3," this ewe was the first mammal ever to have been successfully cloned from an adult cell. Produced at the Roslin Institute in Scotland, "6LL3," or "Dolly,"[20] as she was named by the stockmen who helped with her birth, was cloned by the technique of somatic cell nuclear transfer. Using a cell from an adult sheep's mammary,[21] scientists placed a cell in a denucleated ovum, and waited for the two cells to fuse. Eventually, the fused cells developed into an embryo, and on July 5, 1996, "Dolly" was born.

20. Named for Dolly Parton. Seriously.

21. Tit.

"That sheep absolutely loved to fuck," said Seamus McKracken, a top researcher. "Other sheep. Stockmen. Even the sheep dog. She was insatiable."

Scientists suspect that Dolly's libido was a result of her sense that she only had so much time on this earth. And indeed, she did suffer from shortened telomeres in her cells, which may have been passed on by her "parents." Since Dolly's mother was six years old when the genetic material was taken from her, scientists speculate that *in genetic terms* Dolly was six years old when she was born. She had arthritis by the age of five, lung disease by the age of six, and a bad case of gonorrhea pretty much throughout. Hard facts for Dolly.

PROPAGANDA

I like your Christ. I do not like your Christians.
Your Christians are so unlike your Christ.

—MOHANDAS GANDHI

The Pastafarian Guide to Propaganda

Spreading His Word

NOW THAT YOU KNOW some of the science and history behind Pastafarianism, you may feel that you're ready to go out and spread His Word. With this in mind, it is important to remember that one of the central ideas of FSMism is the idea of *inclusion*. Anyone can be a member, no matter their age, race, background, or even their religious affiliation. As we've stated earlier, we do not base our beliefs on dogma—if we did, we'd have to think that we're absolutely right about everything. Only assholes think that way. And Pastafarians are not assholes.

So remember, Pastafarians are not assholes. We simply deliver His Word and let the people decide.

With inclusion in mind, we feel it is necessary to approach members of other religions in an effort to show them our beliefs. It's possible that Christians, Jews, Muslims, Hindus, Buddhists, and all the other religions, except probably for Scientologists, may be willing to convert after hearing about FSMism. We welcome with open arms any members of other religions. And remember our guarantee:

Try us for thirty days and if you don't like us, your God will most likely take you back.

This is an important detail in spreading His Word. If it works for infomercials, it will definitely work for religion. The God-back guarantee should always be offered *up front*. It shows that we're confident about our beliefs and helps to build trust. Trust is very important when you're trying to change somebody's beliefs. And since we're one of the few religions that's never threatened nonbelievers with violence, it's all we've got.

Before you begin evangelizing, remember to heed this warning:

Be careful of whom you attempt to convert. Members of some religions should be approached with care.

As a missionary you must select a target wisely. Always try to keep to high-traffic areas. That way you can be sure to maximize religious outreach. Always present yourself in a neat and friendly manner, unless you are wearing Pirate regalia, which you should be, in which case you should remember that an eye patch will affect depth perception. This brings us to our next point:

When wearing an eye patch, always remember that objects may be closer or farther away than they appear.

Not only is this statement true in fact, but it is also true spiritually.[1] If you're talking to a Mormon and he keeps smiling pleasantly, be sure to watch his hands. You may think you've cornered a potential Pastafarian, while he may be considering where his gun's at. Always be alert. You are doing His work, but His protective appendages might be occupied with other things. Ask yourself, is this guy taking just a few too many sips of his orange soda? Is one of his wives lurking in the background? If you start to get a bad feeling, leave and live to fight another day. Other religions may be pushy: We're not. In fact, take some hints from Mormons and Jehovah's Witnesses. As much as people like to get visited at home by strangers who tell them they're most likely going to Hell, we prefer less intrusive means of missionary work. Our ways are subtle.

Know your audience and choose the right message.

1. The eye patch is a constant reminder that others don't see the world the same way we do. Not yet, at least.

This is important. Because of the nondogmatic nature of FSMism, there's been some discussion as to whether liberal areas are better for missionary work. Indeed, Pastafarians seem to have good luck finding converts on college campuses, although that could be due to the drugs.[2] Still, there's no doubt that promises of a Beer Volcano and a Stripper Factory in Heaven will likely be more effective with male college students, for example, than with female senior citizens.[3] So always use your noodle and direct the right message to the right audience. A couple of other examples should help:

- ACADEMICS are likely to appreciate that FSMism is based on rigid scientific observations. With them it's a good idea to cite evidence of the Flying Spaghetti Monster's existence. Bring this book along as an aid. Show the academics the pictures, graphs, and diagrams, many of which appear to be scientific in nature. In addition, it may be helpful to note that we Pastafarians are involved in ongoing important research, most importantly related to the established link between global warming and the decline in the Pirate population.

- THE ELDERLY are most easily reached through their firmly entrenched moral values. FSMism is, after all, a comparatively conservative religion. Even though we don't discriminate, and although we openly accept those of varied backgrounds and sexual preference into our religion, it can be noted as advantageous that there are many more gay and lesbian preachers in Christian churches than there are in FSM churches. And while there is nothing particularly important about that phenomenon, it is apparently a big issue with some of the parishioners. So it may be helpful to point out that bit of statistics in order to grow our congregation.[4]

- CHILDREN are generally not the brightest of people, and can be easily converted to FSMism. Mentioning Pirates will ensure it.

- CELEBRITIES are an interesting matter. Consider them to be a special project. When an actor or musician adopts a religion it is a sure sign

2. Might be prudent to try out rehab clinics—Christians have had some success with this, with drug addicts comprising some 90 percent of Born Agains.

3. Possible exception in the ironically named "Bible belt" region of the southern United States, where most older women are well known to be alcoholics and raging lesbians. Source: Jerry Springer.

4. Gay and lesbian people are as welcome as anyone else in our church, and they are also as welcome as their straight counterparts to become clergy.

that it is going to be popular. As such, we suggest identifying one or two hot targets. Lindsay Lohan seems like she'd be open to Pastafarianism. Also, Madonna is probably up for a conversion soon. We suggest approaching those celebrities who appear to be starving. You might want to mention that a high-carbohydrate diet is just what they need to restore their physical and spiritual well-being.

Interacting with Believers of Other Faiths

We will now go through the various faiths and make suggestions for missionaries. As noted above, interacting with other faiths is a touchy subject, as most people who have already found religion believe unquestionably that theirs is the correct one. This is due to the fact that most mainstream religions have successfully convinced their followers that faith—belief not supported by evidence—is a good thing. And so, in the process of converting, say, a Christian to a Pastafarian, not only do you have to convince them to believe in a different God, but you also have to convince them that strong belief without basis, while admittedly more comfortable than thinking, is not our way of doing things. In other words, Pastafarians reject dogma outright. So what it comes down to is that, even if your potential convert accepts the existence of the Flying Spaghetti Monster, he may be unwilling to let go of his dogmatic belief system—having grown accustomed to having his moral values decided for him. It is at the least an uphill battle. That doesn't mean we don't try, though. Pastafarians love a challenge.

Choosing a target takes some psychology. Some religions are more open than others. Luckily, it's not hard to discern what is considered acceptable in each religion. MORMONS, for example, prefer to discuss faith door-to-door with strangers. It follows then that, since this is their chosen method of discourse, they would welcome Pastafarian visitors showing up unannounced at their doorsteps. We suggest arriving as early as possible to make a good impression. Anyone can get up at noon, but it takes dedication and character to make a five A.M. visit. Your potential ex-Mormon/new-Pastafarian converts are likely to notice this and be impressed. It also may not hurt to bring along some orange soda—it's like crack for Mormons. No one knows why exactly, although scientists tell us it probably has something to do with the genetic anomalies caused by generations of endogamous polygamy.

Moving on to CHRISTIANS, it seems that they for the most part don't do door-to-door missionary work, and so we can take a guess that they prefer privacy in their homes. However, it's a different story out in public. Christians can often be found spreading their faith around town, occasionally from elected government positions. We can gather from this that Christians value expressing their faith to the public, and so it follows that they would appreciate this behavior in members of other religions, specifically FSMism.

Take, for instance, a group of Christians on a downtown street corner some Friday night, respectfully protesting passing partygoers with helpful, nonjudgmental signs such as THE PARTY ENDS IN HELL and RE-PENT SINNERS: THE PARTY ENDS IN HELL. These messengers feel so strongly about sharing their interpretation of the Christian faith with strangers that they stand out in the cold for hours. Such open-minded, sharing people are ripe targets for an FSM conversion attempt.

We suggest emulating their behavior as much as possible. Make your own signs, but with our beliefs instead. Think of it as a cultural exchange where both parties can learn about each other's beliefs. And it is a great opportunity to explore differences and similarities for ongoing conversion efforts. For example, our Christian street-corner friends may think beer drinking is wrong, as evidenced by their warnings of eternal hellfire damnation—an obvious but not insurmountable difference from our view, which is that beer rules. And while there may be numerous opposing views such as these, there are going to be some similarities, too. Christians believe in a Heaven—floating on clouds and filled with sunshine and happiness and whatever else—with admission strictly enforced by a judgmental God, morals being a large factor in determining if the new arrival will be let in or instead face an eternal burning lake of fire. Pastafarians also believe in a Heaven, and now you see that we have a similar view that we can build upon. While it's true that the FSM Heaven is thought to be quite different, featuring a Beer Volcano and Stripper Factory, among other attractions, these are details that don't necessarily have to be fully disclosed right away.[5]

Christians make up a large percentage of the world population, so obviously we are going to be dealing with them a lot. The majority of them, unfortunately, are not out evangelizing on street corners, just waiting to be converted. Most are more conservative, preferring only to be told how to think rather than telling others how to think. At first it may seem that this group is ideal to be assimilated into the FSM religion, as we could, in theory, simply tell them new things to think. But remember, FSMism is a fundamentally different type of religion.

We don't tell people how to think, and—we can't say it enough—we reject dogma outright. Our principles preclude us from claiming we know any truths. Instead, we make a strong argument for our beliefs, with the realization that they could be wrong. Our beliefs are based purely on empirical observation, and so it would be dishonest to attempt to convert the conservative dogma-loving Christian populace in this way.

Also, please note that by us claiming that the majority of Christians prefer dogmatic belief to free thought, we are in no way trying to put them down or belittle their beliefs. Dogma admittedly serves a number of functions—primarily societal control—and allows followers to have a rigid set of moral and behavioral guidelines. For many people this is not only comforting but necessary—specifically for Born Agains, the majority of whom would be in jail were it not for the Church's dogmatic message to stop doing crazy shit. I am sure I'm not alone when I say that I'd rather have the Born Agains running the school boards than stealing my car stereo for drug money. So in that respect, dogma is not all bad.

Born Again nuts aside—as far away as possible—many Christians accept the Church for legitimate reasons. In some cases, they truly believe what they're fed as truth, and so it's never an issue. Others accept the Church for the amount of uncomfortable thinking it allows them to avoid. And then there are some Christians who enjoy the social benefits

5. This is accepted practice in matters of religion. Consider the number of Scientologist eunuchs, and how the church wisely avoids mentioning up front the requirement that males donate their testicles a few years after joining.

of a dictated belief system, but at the same time don't actually blindly accept what is presented as incontrovertible truth. These open-minded members are our most likely converts to the Church of FSM. These people will largely not accept the Bible as being literally true—for some reason finding it unlikely, for example, that the first human female was created from a rib, or that the entire earth was flooded. In short, they are Christians but have not been infected with dogma, and so are still able to think freely. They are prime candidates for conversion to FSM.

The problem, of course, is separating the moderate, open-minded Christians from the dogmatic, close-minded ones. Luckily this has already been done for us. We need only visit universities or bookstores, or similar locations—places where independent thought is held in high regard and where intelligent, educated people tend to congregate. There will be very few dogma-minded people here.[6]

These MODERATE CHRISTIANS should require only the minimum of effort to be converted. Being open-minded and intelligent, they will quickly see the benefits of a belief system based on empirical evidence. A religion that holds one of its highest tenets to be the rejection of dogma in its entirety is one not likely to be infested by close-minded fools, and moderate Christians will appreciate this.

The sticking point, perhaps not surprisingly, may be Jesus. An all-but-ready convert who likes the ideology, and probably Pirates as well, may not let herself join because she feels a connection to the Christian Jesus. That's understandable. And remember that it's not our place, as Pastafarians, to tell anyone that their beliefs are wrong. Our role is simply to present our views, not to judge anyone else's views, and certainly not to push our beliefs on others. That being said, it's our duty to make as strong an argument as possible for the Church of the Flying Spaghetti Monster. As such, if you find yourself in a missionary position with a moderate Christian, I think it's appropriate to note that the FSM, being all powerful, could easily have disguised Himself as Jesus and set in place the events that now form the basis of Christianity. If that's the case—and it seems entirely plausible—converting to FSMism would be more consistent with Christianity than worshipping the FSM-placed Christian God.

And lastly, you might ask a moderate Christian a question that they've undoubtedly heard before. What would Jesus do?

We suggest that Jesus would have taken a look at the direction things are going and converted to FSMism. Our beliefs and rejection of dogma are much more consistent with his ideology than much of modern-day dogmatic Christianity. And we find it hard to believe that Jesus would approve of a great deal of the politics enacted ostensibly on his behalf. And he probably wouldn't take kindly to the wars that have been fought in his name either.

WWJD?

HWCTFSM.[7]

7. He Would Convert to FSM.

BORN AGAINS present a different set of challenges. While technically belonging to the Christian faith, they are a separate entity unto themselves. We are hesitant even to refer to them as Christians, because their behavior reflects badly on the majority of Christians who are not insane.

Born Agains are the most dogmatic of all, because it is dogma itself that forms their belief system. The Born Again believes that everyone needs to be told what to do—and realistically, that's the only thing keeping them out of jail. This group has a powerful system of beliefs, and they will tell you about it whenever they get the chance.

Because of their strong dogmatic beliefs, we do not advise going after Born Agains at this time. It is interesting to note, however, that there's only one thing Born Agains enjoy more than telling people what to think, and that is drugs. Some time in the future, after we've completed the construction of our missionary Pirate Ship, we will leave trails of crack vials running from rehab clinics to the port where our Pirate Ship is docked—thus the Born Agains will be led to us, as they gobble up the crack like Pac-Man.

The last Christian group we will consider is the **CHRISTIAN ATHLETE**. These soldiers of God are probably more dangerous than Born Agains due to their size and stamina. They should be avoided at all costs, and only observed on television or watched from the relative safety of your seats set high in the back of an arena or stadium. Christian athletes can be seen praying in the middle of the court, field, or other playing surface after their games, and they are known for thumping their chests and pointing in the air after touchdowns, goals, or "baskets." This unseemly sense of self-importance is disturbing, as God probably doesn't even watch sports.[8] If they think He's actually paying attention when they "give praise" during their interviews, then they're probably even dumber than they sound. As far as the Flying Spaghetti Monster, He is believed only to watch NASCAR and an occasional game of soccer.[9] How else to explain their popularity (NASCAR) and their survival as a professional American sport (soccer)? But we don't know for sure. Again, Christian athletes are highly dangerous and stupid, and should be avoided at all costs.

Now that we've got the Christians covered, we can move on to the other religions. It is important to remember that, regardless of what you hear from many elected officials, there actually are other religions, and they will probably be around for a very long time. Let us explore further.

ISLAM is the world's second largest religion after Christianity. Granted, we don't see a lot of Muslims in this country, but we do see a lot of them on television. It seems that many of them live in places like Iraq and Afghanistan. This is interesting to note, because some of our greatest missionary work is taking place in these places, where there are a surprising number of Pastafarians in the military. While people believe that the president sent troops into Iraq to find WMDs, it's pretty much been common knowledge that most of the weapons they were supposedly looking for were over in Iran and North Korea. So why did he send so many troops to the wrong country? As you know, until recently, Iraq was a country run by a secular government, under the rule of Saddam Hussein.[10] High government officials in the United States predicted correctly that it would be easier to convert a secular country to Pastafarianism than it would be to convert, say, Iran. This program of bringing His Word to the people has been termed by the Pentagon as Operation Wiggly

8. If anything, He should be paying attention to the news.

9. See Diego Maranara's "Noodle of God." Argentina vs. England, June 22, 1986.

10. Although Saddam does kind of resemble a Pirate, he most certainly is not a Pastafarian.

Multiappendaged Deity, or Operation WMD for short. As President Bush probably once said, "We are making progress in Iraq. But it's going to take time." Tune in to see how it goes.

HINDUISM is another big religion. There are millions and millions of Hindus in India. You might just show a Hindu a picture of a typical Hindu god to illustrate the extreme noodliness of his appendages. That should work.

BUDDHISM, like FSMism, is a highly peaceful religion. Buddhists practice much meditation, and we suggest that the best way to allow for them to be touched by His Noodly Appendage is simply to share His favorite meal. After a couple of healthy portions of pasta, watch the Buddhist slip into a food coma, which is very much like experiencing meditation. When he comes out of it, he will most certainly have received enlightenment.

JEWS are an interesting group to consider. They're certainly a driven bunch, often highly educated and well connected. For the highly educated Jews, simply follow the advice given above under "Academics." They will enjoy the empirical evidence that we provide them, and will surely adopt Pastafarianism for themselves. For Orthodox

Jews, point out the tzitzit[11] that they wear. Moses himself was told to wear one, and the strings do resemble His Noodly Appendages, so we can only assume that the Flying Spaghetti Monster made the suggestion in the first place. Those trendy Kabbalists wear red strings around their wrists to ward off the evil eye. Red is the color of His sauce, and string is the shape of His spaghetti, proving that even Madonna has been touched by His Noodly Appendage.

11. A traditional garment with long trailing strings.

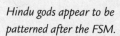

Hindu gods appear to be patterned after the FSM.

JAINISM is perhaps the ultimate pacifist religion. They don't believe in violence of any kind. They only eat vegetables. Some of them don't even wear clothes. They're like the three-toed sloths of religious people. Approach them slowly, for they're known to spontaneously burst into tears. Talk to them quietly about our nonviolent and all-inclusive policies. Don't mention the Pirates. Offer them some vegetable Ramen. The Jains are often starving and will appreciate the food.

SHINTOISM is the official religion of Japan.[12] Yet it's interesting to note that a large percentage of Japanese people practice both Shintoism and Buddhism. This makes Shintoists an easy target. Simply suggest that they adopt a third religion: Pastafarianism. Again, offer them some Ramen. Japanese people love it.

12. Coincidentally, Japan is the official country of Ramen.

RASTAFARIANS are loosely organized and not particularly widespread. Because a large concentration of Rastafarians lives in the Caribbean, a key habitat of Pirates, Pastafarians and Rastafarians appear to intermingle quite well. The best thing to do when converting Rastafarians is to wait. Once they've got the munchies, offer them some Ramen. Mention how the two religions rhyme. Point to Bob Marley's dreadlocks and compare them to the Noodly Appendaged FSM. We actually believe that most Rastafarians are Pastafarians already.

SCIENTOLOGISTS are best left alone.

In summary, there are several ways to spread His Word. Depending on the location, it might be safer to post flyers, posters, brochures, etc., rather than confronting strangers. However, while anonymously planted flyers and brochures may convert a few people, they're probably not enough to convert those with a more skeptical mind. Our religion is, after all, admittedly hard to believe at first. But no one ever said that faith was easy, and having several packs of delicious, ready-to-cook Ramen around you at all times will help. Person-to-person evangelizing is a necessary method of outreach, as there are some people who will not allow themselves to be touched by His Noodly Appendage unless you're right there, putting it in their face.

A Final Note from Bobby Regarding Midgets

I can honestly say that I've received much more flak over the term *midgets* from fully grown (oftentimes fat) people than from "little people" themselves. One could make the argument that the little person community[13] itself is not concerned with such petty matters of political correctness. And while that is a valid and probable explanation, in the name of full disclosure, I would like to note that my hearing is not the best, and that if an angry little person has ever confronted me over the term *midget*, I may not have noticed, as I generally look straight ahead. At any rate, until such time as a little person himself asks me to stop,[14] I will continue to use the term *midget* as often as possible.

13. Located primarily at the North Pole.

14. I suggest either a sign firmly attached to a meter stick, or in the unlikely but awesome occasion of two little people, please consider sitting atop the other's shoulders. I absolutely guarantee my full attention in this case.

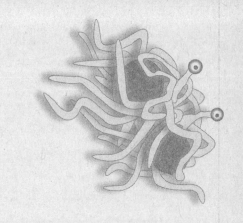

Pamphlets

As intrepid soldiers of the FSM, we come armed only with our faith,
numerous examples of observable evidence, and maybe some
Ramen or placards. In addition, we have pamphlets, which reduce
our message to easily digestible sound bites. Turn the page and
read on. Feel free to copy these pamphlets for your own
evangelical work. Consider them to be
extensions of His Noodly message.

RAmen

FLYING SPAGHETTI MONSTERISM
Have you been touched by His Noodly Appendage?

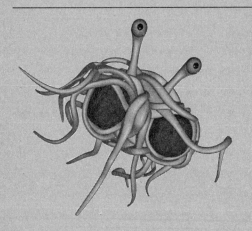

THE CHURCH OF THE FLYING SPAGHETTI MONSTER

There are multiple theories of Intelligent Design. Many people around the world are of the strong belief that the universe was created by a Flying Spaghetti Monster. It was He who created all that we see and all that we feel. We feel strongly that the overwhelming scientific evidence pointing toward Evolutionary processes is nothing but a coincidence, put in place by Him.

WHAT ELSE SHOULD I KNOW?

We have evidence that a Flying Spaghetti Monster created the universe. None of us, of course, were around to see it, but we have written accounts of it. We have several lengthy volumes explaining all details of His power. Also, you may be surprised to hear that there

are over ten million of us, and growing. We tend to be very secretive, as many people claim our beliefs are not substantiated by observable evidence.

SCIENTIFIC PROOF

He built the world to make us think the earth is older than it really is. For example, a scientist may perform a carbon-dating process on an artifact. He finds that approximately 75 percent of the carbon-14 had decayed by electron emission to nitrogen-14, and infers that this artifact is approximately 10,000 years old, as the half-life of carbon-14 appears to be 5,730 years. But what our scientist does not realize is that every time he makes a measurement, the Flying Spaghetti Monster is there changing the results with His Noodly Appendage. We have numerous texts that describe in detail how this can be possible and the reasons why He does this. He is, of course, invisible and can pass through normal matter with ease.

MORE PROOF WITH A GRAPH!!

You may be interested to know that global warming, earthquakes, hurricanes, and other natural disasters are a direct result of the shrinking number of Pirates since the 1800s.

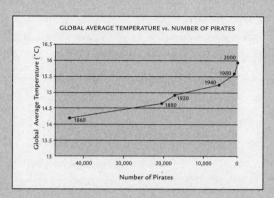

GLOBAL AVERAGE TEMPERATURE vs. NUMBER OF PIRATES

The graph above shows the approximate number of Pirates versus the average global temperature over the last two hundred years. As you can see, there is a statistically significant inverse relationship between Pirates and global temperature.

WHAT DOES THIS MEAN?

We are sure you now realize how important it is that this alternate theory is spread. It is absolutely imperative that everyone realizes that observable evidence is at the discretion of the Flying Spaghetti Monster. Furthermore, it is disrespectful to teach our beliefs without wearing His chosen outfit, which, of course, is full Pirate regalia. I cannot stress the importance of this enough, and unfortunately cannot describe in detail why this must be done as we have run out of space. The concise explanation is that He becomes angry if we don't.

CONCLUSION

Thank you for taking the time to read about our views and beliefs. We hope this pamphlet was able to convey the importance of teaching this theory to our children and to everyone. We can all look forward to the time when the three theories of creation are given equal time in our science classrooms across the country, and eventually the world: one third time for Intelligent Design, one third time for Flying Spaghetti Monsterism, and one third time for logical conjecture based on overwhelming observable evidence.

"If Intelligent Design is taught in schools, equal time should be given to the FSM theory and the non-FSM theory."

—Douglas Shaw, Ph.D.

"Do not be hypocritical. Allow equal time for other alternative 'theories' like FSMism, which is by far the tastier choice."

—J. Simon, Ph.D.

"In my scientific opinion when comparing the two theories, FSM theory seems to be more valid than the classic ID theory."

—Afshin Beheshti, Ph.D.

WHAT THE EXPERTS ARE SAYING

"As a scientist, I'd like to say that the currently accepted scientific theory is Evolution. But some competing ideas have been proposed, such as ID and FSMism, and discussion to include one should include the other, as these ideas are equally valid."

—*Mark Zurbuchen, Ph.D.*

"It seems to me the FSM theory is MUCH more plausible than the non-FSM ID theory, because it is the only one of the two that takes into account all the discrepancies between ID and measurable objective reality."

—*Douglas Shaw, Ph.D*

"All points of view should be available to students studying the origins of mankind."

—*Senator John McCain*

"[Evolution] is not a fact. . . . We're dealing with censorship here. If we only taught Shakespeare in English class, that wouldn't be fair."

—*Senator Chris Buttars*

"At one time, I believed as the Aztecs did, that the universe was created by two gods, Quetzalcoatl and Tezcatlipoca, who attacked and ripped apart Hungry Woman to create the universe. Then I believed, as the Moriori do, that the universe was created when Papa and her husband Rangi hugged and bore children. . . . However, my views have been swayed by . . . the Flying Spaghetti Monster (FSM). I am firmly convinced that the evidence . . . has many of the trappings of science, and I therefore support the inclusion of FSM creation evidence in the Kansas science curriculum and standards."

—*Sebastian Wren, Ph.D.*

"MMMMMmmmmm, spaghetti."

—*H. Neville, Ph.D.*

WHY YOU SHOULD CONVERT TO FLYING SPAGHETTI MONSTERISM

- Flimsy moral standards.
- Every Friday is a religious holiday.
- Our Heaven is WAY better. We've got a Stripper Factory AND a Beer Volcano.

WE ARE ALL HIS CREATURES

- How was the universe created?
- What is the origin of species?
- Why does empirical evidence seem to support theories like Evolution, gravity, and quantum mechanics?
- Why has the earth seen an increase in global warming, earthquakes, hurricanes, and other natural disasters since the 1800s?
- What's with the full Pirate regalia?

Open up for the answers to these questions and more!

TOUCHED BY HIS NOODLY APPENDAGE

EXCERPTED FROM BOBBY HENDERSON'S OPEN LETTER TO THE KANSAS SCHOOL BOARD

I am writing to you with much concern after having read of your hearing to decide whether the alternative theory of Intelligent Design should be taught along with the theory of Evolution . . .

Let us remember that there are multiple theories of Intelligent Design. I and many others around the world are of the strong belief that **the universe was created by a Flying Spaghetti Monster.** It was He who created all that we see and all that we feel. We feel strongly that the overwhelming scientific evidence pointing toward Evolutionary processes is nothing but a coincidence, put in place by Him.

It is for this reason that I'm writing to you today, to formally request that this alternative theory be taught in your schools, along with the other two theories. If the Intelligent Design theory is not based on faith but on another scientific theory, as is claimed, then you must also allow our theory to be taught, as it is also based on science, not on faith.

Some find that hard to believe, so it may be helpful to tell you a little more about our beliefs. We have evidence that a Flying Spaghetti Monster created the universe. None of us, of course, were around to see it, but we have written accounts of it. We have several lengthy volumes explaining all details of His power. Also, you may be surprised to hear that there are over ten million of us, and growing. We tend to be very secretive, as many people claim our beliefs are not substantiated by observable evidence. What these people don't understand is that **He built the world to make us think the earth is older than it really is.** For example, a scientist may perform a carbon-dating process on an artifact. He finds that approximately 75 percent of the carbon-14 has decayed by electron emission to nitrogen-14, and infers that this artifact is approximately 10,000 years old, as the half-life of carbon-14 appears to be 5,730 years. But what our scientist does not realize is that every time he makes a measurement, the Flying Spaghetti Monster is there changing the results with His Noodly Appendage. We have numerous texts that describe in detail how this can be possible and the reasons why He does this. He is, of course, invisible and can pass through normal matter with ease.

I'm sure you now realize how important it is that your students are taught this alternate theory. It is absolutely imperative that they realize that observable evidence is at the discretion of the Flying Spaghetti Monster.

Furthermore, it is disrespectful to teach our beliefs without wearing His chosen outfit, which of course is full Pirate regalia. I cannot stress the importance of this enough, and unfortunately cannot describe in detail why this must be done as I fear this letter is already becoming too long. The concise explanation is that He becomes angry if we don't.

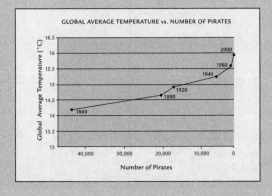

You may be interested to know that global warming, earthquakes, hurricanes, and other natural disasters are a direct effect of the shrinking number of Pirates since the 1800s. For your interest, I have included a graph of the approximate number of Pirates versus the average global temperature over the last two hundred years. As you can see, there is a statistically significant inverse relationship between Pirates and global temperature.

I am eagerly awaiting your response, and hope dearly that no legal action will need to be taken. I think we can all look forward to the time when these three theories are given equal time in our science classrooms across the country, and eventually the world; one-third time for Intelligent Design, one-third time for Flying Spaghetti Monsterism, and one-third time for logical conjecture based on overwhelming observable evidence.

Smart People Who Agree with Us

"One of the most exciting developments in physics recently is so-called string theory, in which all subatomic particles are described as microscopic vibrating strings. Obviously this is correct, though misnamed. As Noodle Theory reveals, He has created the matter in the universe in His own quivering image! You, me, the earth, the stars . . . are all built of trillions of tiny jiggling noodles, microscopic copies of our diving saucy maker. Boy-oh-Boyardi and Ramen!"

—*Steve Lawrence, Ph.D.*

"Having now perused the many facets of Pastafarianism, I believe there is great scope for women in this religion. Clearly the FSM has aspects of both male and female, with both 'Noodly Appendages' and two round meatballs, which clearly represent the breasts of the Great Mother Goddess."

—*Susan Johnston, Ph.D.*

"As a neuroscientist and clinical psychologist, I have often been struck by how the brain resembles pasta. Clearly, the FSM theory is worthy of deep thought. Or at least a side order of garlic toast. Which is more than I can say about ID, which, as St. Sigmund taught, should be subservient to EGO (equally goofy observations)."

—*James Blackburn, Ph.D.*

"Pastafarianism does not constitute a scientific theory, despite its apparent adherence to Heisenberg's uncertainty principle regarding the interactions of observer and observed. It should not be taught as science . . . unless, of course, ID creationism is also taught as science, in which case all bets are off. Best of luck, I'm off to the Old Spaghetti Factory for worship."

—*E. Scott*

The Ontological Argument for FMS

P1. The Flying Spaghetti Monster is a being that has every perfection.
P2. Existence is a perfection.
C. Therefore, the Flying Spaghetti Monster exists.

FOR MORE INFORMATION AND TO LEARN HOW YOU CAN HELP, PLEASE GO TO

www.venganza.org

How to Make Your Own Pirate-Fish Stencil

SUPPLIES

Razor blade or X-Acto knife

Thin cardboard

Tape

Spray paint

Cut out the template at the back of this book.

Tape the template to a piece of thin cardboard.

Cut out the Pirate Fish. Don't forget a small line for the nostrils!

Completed stencil.

Hold the stencil firmly against the surface you want to tag and spray paint.

Spread the word in interesting places.

How to Make Your Very Own
Flying Spaghetti Monster Simulacrum

SUPPLIES

    Two googly eyes

    One bag of rubber bands (about 50)

    One pipe cleaner

    Two brown fluff balls

    Glue

    Scissors

The FSM simulacrum consists of one noodly loop, two noodly strands and two eyestalks. It is best first to glue the googly eyes to the pipe cleaner, then the glue can dry while you make the Noodly Appendages.

To begin the creation, you must first make a noodly loop by cutting several rubber bands and tying them onto an uncut band.

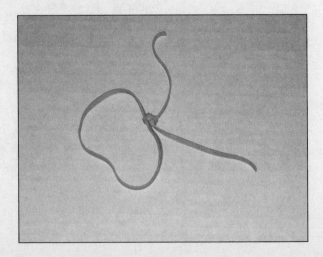

A completed
noodly loop.

Here is the tricky part. Use
one cut band to tie the
noodly loop to the pipe
cleaner. Tie it so that it
pinches the loop in the
middle, creating two loops
that the fluff balls can later
be inserted into.

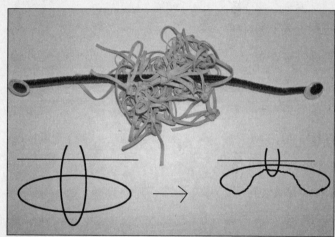

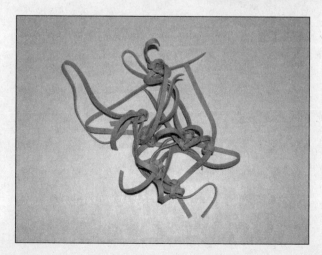

The noodly strands are
made exactly the same way
as the noodly loops, except
that you tie the uncut bands
onto a cut band instead of
an uncut one. Use fewer
bands for a noodly strand
and concentrate them at the
end of the cut band. Use
about eight bands.

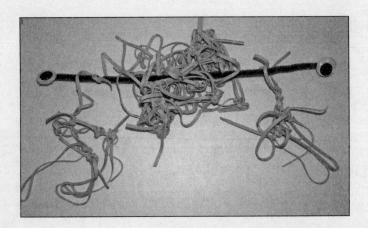

Tie the noodly strands to the pipe cleaner, one on each side of the noodly loop.

Insert the fluff balls into the sides of the noodly loop.

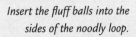

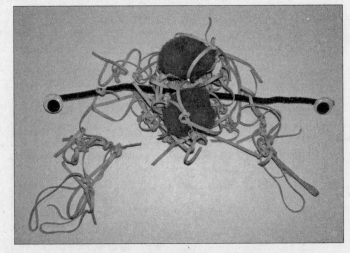

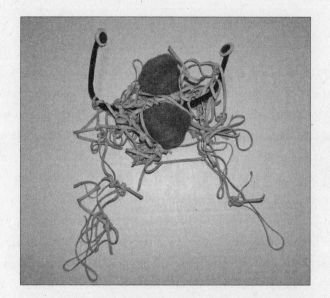

Bend the pipe cleaner to make the eyestalks. If your noodly strands hang down too low, you may need to tie them up at the middle.

The completed FSM simulacrum.

Fund-raising

NEVITABLY, THE MATTER OF MONEY will come up, and many will find it hard to believe that FSM is a free religion: Indeed, no tithing is expected. Apparently our God is in a better financial position than Jesus, just to name an example. Churches are expensive, obviously, and ours—a Pirate Ship[1] —will require more upkeep than a conventional church, but the funds will come from unsolicited donations rather than expected contributions. No Pastafarian will ever endure the expectant look of a collection-holding, blue-haired old bat, as is customary among some of the other major religions. If members don't want to contribute to the cause, they don't have to. Freeloaders will be welcome aboard the Ship—however they most certainly will not be allowed to touch the cannons. There has to be some motivation to contribute, after all.

Still, we are not above devising certain fund-raising schemes to ensure that we can obtain as big and as glorious a Pirate Ship as possible. The sale of T-shirts helps. Also, coffee mugs and bumper stickers are effective. But FSMism is a highly international and Web savvy church, and we seek to utilize those attributes to bring in a particularly big windfall.

Our idea for a major new fund-raising campaign involves time travel and the lottery. Ever since the world was discovered to be round, scientists and explorers have known that there are times when it is Tuesday in one place yet it remains Monday somewhere else. We plan on turning this often ignored fact to our advantage. By using super-fast Internet connections, we will have foreign Pastafarians on, say, Tuesday morning look up what the winning lottery numbers were and send them back to us where it's still Monday (i.e., in the past). This scheme will require a lot of cooperation on the part of Pastafarians, and we are certainly up to the task. While some may question the ethics of such a plan, we argue that our ethical standards are rock solid when compared to televangelical Christians who garner a fair amount of their wealth from recently cashed Social Security checks.

1. ETA 2007.

A Guide to the Holidays

hile all days spent as a Pastafarian are indeed glorious, there are a few very special days, commonly known as "holidays," when we celebrate His Noodly Presence.[1]

PASTOVER is a religious holiday analogous to the Jewish holiday of Passover, as well as the Christian holiday of Easter. During this time, Pastafarians across the globe are encouraged to eat copious amounts of pasta, usually spaghetti, which is cooked "in His image" by family members dressed as Pirates. Pastover celebrates the time when the Flying Spaghetti Monster first began touching people with His Noodly Appendage. Many stories about this momentous occasion have been passed down through the centuries, and it is interesting to note that they are all completely different. Some are hardly even intelligible. Regardless of one's version of the story, however, all true believers partake of the pasta and perform the ritual Passing of the Eye Patch, in which each member at the table takes a turn wearing an eye patch and talking about why he or she is happy to have been touched.

1. Quite a number of days are dedicated to saints of the Church of the Flying Spaghetti Monster. Although they will not be mentioned in this section, we should correct one troubling misunderstanding: Chef Boyardee is *not* a saint and, in fact, may not even be a real person.

RAMENDAN is analogous to the Islamic period of fasting, prayer, and charity known as Ramadan. Ramendan comes around the same time as Ramadan, and indeed the two holiday periods have their similarities. One of the major differences between the two, however, is that Pastafarians do not fast or pray, as doing so would conflict with their flimsy moral standards. Instead, Pastafarians spend a few days of the month eating only Ramen noodles and remembering back to their days as starving college students. This simple act teaches

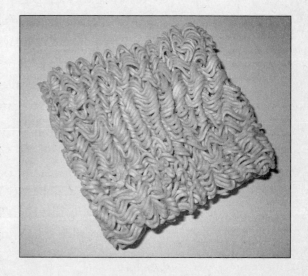

Pastafarians to be happy about what they've accomplished, and if they haven't accomplished anything yet, to at least be happy that they are Pastafarians. Ramendan is the least commercial of the Pastafarian holidays, which is saying a lot, since you aren't going to see a Pastover sale at Macy's any time soon. At the end of Ramendan, Pastafarians are encouraged to give their extra Ramen to those who are more needy.

HALLOWEEN is an important Pastafarian holiday because it honors the time when Pirates roamed the earth in freedom. Pirates were His Chosen People, and their dwindling numbers have had a direct effect on the world around us. It can be safely assumed that the recent spate of earthquakes, hurricanes, and other natural disasters, as well as the advent of global warming, can all be traced back to the alarming decrease in Pirates worldwide. Pastafarians often dress up as Pirates on Halloween and pass out candy to children. Indeed, it is a little known fact that the original Pirates were well known for passing out candy to children, but that practice grew less common as they became persecuted. During Halloween, Pastafarians are urged to travel their neighborhoods, if not the Seven Seas, in search of wenches and grog.

INTERNATIONAL TALK LIKE A PIRATE DAY takes place every September 19 and is a fine day for Pastafarians to celebrate their Pirate roots. Much like Halloween, Pastafarians are encouraged to seek out wenches and grog on this holiday; candy is optional. It should also be noted that International Talk Like a Pirate Day might be a good time for evangelical work, as grog weakens even the most hardened mind and makes people more open to alternative viewpoints like Pastafarianism. It is estimated that one half of annual conversions to the Church of the Flying Spaghetti Monster take place on this day.

FRIDAY is the holiest of the Pastafarian holidays and takes place each week. During this High Day, Pastafarians are encouraged to take it easy and, if possible, try to find some sun. Fridays are dedicated to the ideals beholden in the Beer Volcano and the Stripper Factory, and one can do no more to honor His Noodly Appendage than to observe Fridays with the utmost of piety.

HOLIDAY encompasses pretty much all of the big commercial holidays celebrated by the other religions. Holiday stretches over most of December and January, and it is interesting to consider how much this Pastafarian religion has spread over the last couple of years. In fact, many schools and businesses refer not to the "Christmas season," but to the Pastafarian "Holiday season" instead. This is strong evidence of our rapid growth, and we feel that a special thanks should go out to Wal-Mart, who rejected the Christian phrase "Merry Christmas" in favor of the Pastafarian greeting "Happy Holidays." We appreciate your support.

Enlightenment Institute

PASTAFARIANS DON'T REST ON THEIR LAURELS. Sure we've got lots of proofs already, but we can never truly stop our effort to spread His Word (unless it's a Friday).

String theory—all matter is created of little noodlelike strings. Coincidence?

Bacteria flagella—can anything that complex and noodlelike have happened by accident? Heresy.

But obviously we need more evidence of His existence, and so we have established the Enlightenment Institute—a think tank devoted to proving our a priori assumption that He exists, using all available specious arguments and circular logic to do so. In case you haven't been paying attention, this approach is totally legit in matters of religion, and has gained increased legitimacy in politicized science. This important work has been taken up by some of the greatest minds available to us.

What follows are proofs that have been submitted to the Enlightenment Institute's publishing arm, the *Science Creative Quarterly*, the first science publication to take notice of the obvious legitimacy of FSM. They are the rare and hard-won fruits of some of the greatest thinkers at work in the world today.

The Case for the Church of the Immaculate Induction

Kelly Black

DEPARTMENT OF MATHEMATICS

UNION COLLEGE, SCHENECTADY, NY

ABSTRACT

Recent political efforts to broaden the scope of science education and bring science into the mainstream have generated a great deal of controversy. One of the things that has been sorely missing is the relationship between mathematics and religion. Here we attempt to inject a greater mathematical essence into religion as well as explore one immediate implication, the immaculate induction hypothesis.

INTRODUCTION We focus on the injection of a greater mathematical sensibility within the religious community and examine the resulting implications. In doing so we agree that Intelligent Design is a valid viewpoint, but ask what this implies. We find that this implies a countable sequence of all-powerful and all-knowing entities going back through all time. The basic argument is that the complexity of the known universe implies the existence of a creator. The union of the creator and creation is a set that is more complex than just the universe and thus implies a creator of the larger set. An induction hypothesis follows readily from this approach.

The motivation for this work comes from recent efforts to inject the ideas of Intelligent Design into the science curriculum, which has generated enormous attention in the mainstream media. Unfortunately, both sides accuse the other of being close-minded. In this game of tug of war both sides must be recalcitrant in order for the game to continue.

The current situation comes as little surprise to those of us in the mathematics community. We have been well aware of the proclivities of both sides. We have been long-time observers of both sides and have noted these tendencies for many millennia. The mathematics community itself is also composed of people who share most of the traits of both sides—dogmatic, religious fervor combined with supreme arrogance—

and we watch this terrible conflict with an awful understanding of the pain felt on both sides.

It is for this very reason that the mathematics community can no longer sit on the sideline. In particular we address the need for a greater mathematical ethic within the religious community through a preliminary investigation of Intelligent Design. This may seem one-sided, but the close relationship that has developed between the mathematics and science communities (with the exceptions of chemistry, biology, geology, and psychology) is already well documented and subject to intense scrutiny.

THE GENESIS STORY

There has always been some tension between science and religion. Ironically, this tension has been seemingly focused on minor issues. The trial over Galileo's assertion that the earth revolves around the sun relies on a single, ambiguous statement within the Old Testament. Men of great intellect and passion clashed over a trivial statement that has since been all but forgotten.

We now find ourselves with a similar clash. We are focused on the story of our origin. Again the clash centers on a relatively minor aspect of a broad tale. This time it is the Genesis story that is at the center of the conflict. One might think that the Genesis story is really about the gift given to us by the creator. This is the gift of creation but more importantly the gift of free will. We were given creation and allowed the freedom to experience it on our own terms with all of the associated responsibilities.

It is easy to think that the story of Genesis comes down to the simple message that it is immoral to force particular beliefs onto others. Such a simple interpretation ignores the powerful draw of the story of our origin. It is the story of our origin that has become the focal point of conflict. The primordial draw of the question of our origin drives us in a way that is beyond reason or explanation.

The sacred texts of Christianity, Judaism, Islam, and all other religions provide numerous examples about the relationships between the weak and the powerful, the rich and the poor, and provide explicit guidance on how we should treat one another. Rather than focus on such simple ideals that are already clearly articulated within each of the sacred texts, we focus on the much more difficult and important story of our origin.

THE MATHEMATICS OF THE CREATOR

Our only way of studying the creator is to examine creation. The universe is a collection of simple objects that when brought together represent a staggering set of interactions. We are capable of studying and generating a basic understanding of small parts but are incapable of understanding the whole. For example, while sitting within this goldfish bowl we call "earth," light seemingly strikes us that appears to have been generated millions of years ago by events taking place on spatial scales beyond our understanding. At the same time, the molecular kinetics of proteins within our own cells exhibit nonlinear, chaotic oscillations that, taken together, create the reliable, stable clockwork that makes life possible. This complexity implies the existence of a creator.

All things around us have been created, and we denote creation as the "universe" or more formally as U_0. That which initiated the creation of U_0 has the full power and understanding of all that is within U_0. All that is within us and beyond us is contained in U_0 and thus is a part of the understanding and abilities of the creator. At the same time the creator, denoted C_0, is an integral part of creation. The two do not stand apart but rather are part of the unity of the Grand Design. Taken together we denote the union of C_0 and U_0 as G_0.

From where did G_0 arise? The subtle interactions found within U_0 imply the existence of C_0. The cardinality of G_0 is greater than or equal to the cardinality of U_0, since $C_0 \in G_0$. We find that a creator, denoted C_1, must exist as that can explain the intricacies of G_0. From the existence of C_1, we find that G_0 must be contained within another universe composed of all that created by C_1, which we denote U_1.

It is possible that U_1 is equal to G_0 but it is not necessary. Hence we have that $G_0 \subseteq U_1$. We now have the basis for our induction hypothesis: C_1 initiated U_1. We denote the union of these two sets, $C_1 \cup U_1$, as G_1. Since the cardinality of G_1 is greater than or equal to the cardinality of U_1, which was created by C_1, there must exist a C_2 that can explain the intricacies and complexities of G_1.

Proceeding in this way, we must conclude in the existence of G_2. Applying the same reasoning implies the existence of a countable set, G_i, where $G_i \subseteq G_{i+1}$ and associated with each G_i is a creator, C_i. We leave the formal statement and proof of the immaculate induction hypothesis as an exercise for the reader.

Finally, this construction of G_i leads to a fascinating array of corollaries such as

$$G_0 = \lim_{n \to \infty} \bigcap_{i=0}^{n} G_i$$

that we do not explore here. We leave these as work to be completed with hopes that they will provide an enormous draw to this new and fascinating field of study.

Conclusion

In this paper we examine the mathematics of creation and uncover just one implication, the immaculate induction hypothesis. The availability of the power of mathematical analysis helps make clear the connections between the sacred and the profane. In this one example we examine the implication of just one simple religious truth, the complexity and beauty of the world around us imply the existence of a creator, C_0.

Through this one example we readily see that the power of mathematical analysis is a necessary component of any complete religious education and makes the case that greater mathematical content be added to the religion curriculum. This is necessary because the practice of religious study requires the communication of complex ideals with intricate interactions. Religious dialogue requires that we discuss and share the nature of infinite love and the infinite universe. In doing so it simply is not possible to share the full spectrum of the sacred without the language of mathematics.

Put simply, it is self-evident that the nature of religious dialogue has all the hallmarks of a hidden Grand Design. The intense and complicated interactions of nearly all human thought hide an underlying intelligence that can only be explained by the presence of an intrinsic, hidden mathematical structure.

A Teleological Argument

Landon W. Rabern

DEPARTMENT OF MATHEMATICS

UC SANTA BARBARA

PROPOSITION 1. The universe exhibits too much structure to have evolved by chance.

CONCLUSION 1. There was a creator.

PROPOSITION 2. All things are subject to the passage of time.

CONCLUSION 2. The processes of the universe were in action over the time period in which it was created.

PROPOSITION 3. Nothing, not even a God, can know the exact outcome of a situation in the universe. Moreover, the uncertainty increases with the time elapsed since the parameters of the situation were known.

CONCLUSION 3. If the creator wished to make the universe precisely as he pleased, then he would need to do it rapidly.

PROPOSITION 4. Any being that would create a universe for his pleasure is an egotistical maniac.

CONCLUSION 4. The creator was an egotistical maniac.

CONCLUSION 5. Since an egotistical maniac would want things done his way, he must have, by C3, made the universe extremely rapidly; in fact, as rapidly as possible.

PROPOSITION 5. If a creator could affect more points of space simultaneously, then he could create the structure in the universe more rapidly.

CONCLUSION 6. A creator with more appendages than another could have created the universe more rapidly.

CONCLUSION 7. Since, by C5, the creator made the universe as rapidly as possible, he has as many appendages as possible.

PROPOSITION 6. The universe is discrete.

CONCLUSION 8. There is a minimal thickness to the appendages of a creator.

CONCLUSION 9. A creator with thinner appendages can have more of them.

CONCLUSION 10. By C7 and C9, the creator had as many appendages as possible, all of minimal thickness.

CONCLUSION 11. The creator was a Flying Spaghetti Monster.

Proof of Proposition 3:

PROPOSITION 7. The creator made us for his pleasure.

PROPOSITION 8. There is no pleasure to be drawn from us if we do not have free will.

CONCLUSION 12. We have free will.

PROPOSITION 9. If the universe was predetermined, then we would not have free will.

CONCLUSION 13. The universe is not predetermined.

PROPOSITION 10. The creator set up the initial conditions of the universe.

CONCLUSION 14. By C13, there is uncertainty in the unfolding of the universe.

CONCLUSION 15. As uncertainty on top of uncertainty brings even more uncertainty, as time passes, the level of uncertainty increases.

CONCLUSION 16. Proposition 3 is true.

RAmen.

Of Penguins and Pasta
Toby Leonard with editing by Jason Braunwarth
HISTORIAN, SCHOLAR, AND ALL-AROUND SWELL GUY

There is irrevocable proof that the Flying Spaghetti Monster (FSM) created the world. Some people point to selective fossil evidence and then use fuzzy interpolation to explain gaps in the fossil record, some use fictitious supreme beings, and others claim some Intelligent Designer created everything. I have factual proof that on every continent all that was created was touched by His Noodly Appendage. Others point to esoteric folklore to explain "their God," but the FSM has touched every continent and every culture, leaving His mark with His Noodly Appendage. To clarify this overwhelming preponderance of evidence I shall break this down by continent to make it understandable to even the densest dogmatist. To start, I shall strike at the legendary home of the WASP, Europe.

Europe is the simplest example of the great work of the FSM. We can easily bear witness to the numerous pastas attributed to Italy, where one finds the origin of the contemporary name "Flying Spaghetti Monster" in the pasta called "spaghetti." This long thin cylindrical pasta is not the only pasta on the menu; the types and shapes vary tremendously and the sauces that accompany them bring the selection to heavenly proportions. This is the most commonly cited example of evidence for the FSM, but there is evidence implying His existence before Italy discovered pasta. Certain geographical features are even named after Him. The Danube River is a perfect example: It is simply the old Hungarian term for "Da Noodle River." Even the uppity French have unquestionable Stone Age fossil evidence of His work in the "Acheulean Stone Twirling Spaghetti Fork" from Saint-Acheul, France, which has been dated approximately 1,000,000 to 300,000 B.C.E. From this we can gather unquestionable evidence of His hand in human cultures dating back as far as one million years.

Europe, while first discussed in this essay, is not the starting point of Pastafarian history. Africa, the birthplace of humanity, is a continent that is only beginning to be discovered by Pastafarian archaeologists, its potential for providing incontrovertible evidence of the Noodly One's manipulations is only recently being realized. This minor oversight of the archaeological community is exemplified by the presence of only two significant facts of historical record. The first is the presence of their own version of pasta, the Moroccan couscous, which was obviously manna from Heaven and its abundance and shape is reflective of the environment in which it is eaten. Couscous is shaped in the likeness of sand, to match the sandy desert environment in which the early Moroccans lived. This is an example of how the FSM is kind and understanding of the people in giving them a gift of pasta to which they can relate. Without an example of stringy spaghetti in the habitat, the people would not have known what to do with stringy noodles, so the FSM shaped their pasta to match that of sand and instructed the locals to eat it. Now great sand dunes can be looked upon as manna from Heaven in the form of huge piles of couscous. The second example is from ancient Egypt. Due to a mistake in translations from the Rosetta Stone, the word for "reed" was substituted for "Megaghetti" (a large diameter form of spaghetti), thus the hieroglyphs were incorrectly interpreted as showing people gathering reeds instead of making huge bundles of megaghetti. The Phoenicians were said to have made reed boats to sail the seas, and everyone knows this is impossible. Anyone would know that megaghetti boats would self-seal in a pasty mass when contacting the warm ocean waters, producing a leakproof, seaworthy vessel. It is through these original megaghetti boats that trade in the Mediterranean Sea was started. So we see that from Africa, the FSM touched the desert people and started major trading empires. We shall go across the Atlantic to the New World empires.

South America had great ancient civilizations. They had gold galore, they had yams, chocolate, potatoes, corn, cocaine, calendars that needed a leap day every few hundred years, extensive agriculture, and a huge bureaucracy. However, they lacked three important things required in any ancient civilization: They never utilized the wheel, they didn't have horses, and they had no pasta. The shame of not being able to roll or ride was bad enough, but to not eat pasta pulled at the very fabric of society. Both the Incas and the Aztecs tried to make up for these shortcomings. They conquered natives, they collected gold, they made temples, they pleaded to inferior gods, but nothing they tried worked. In desperation they started sacrificing humans to appease the inferior gods in hopes of gaining the great knowledge of noodles to guide them. This gambit was doomed to fail, and the arrival of Cortez hastened this failure. Some scholars claimed it was smallpox that wiped out Montezuma's armies, but that was not the case. Cortez brought not smallpox, but a small tin of SpaghettiOs. Montezuma, realizing his own lack of SpaghettiOs, ordered his troops to fall upon their swords in shame. Ninety-seven percent of the population committed suicide, for their inability to attain enlightenment and noodles caused them desperation and abject shame. The other 3 percent were shameless cowards. Cortez, never one to shy away from credit, be it earned or not, claimed to have conquered the nation for Spain and gathered up the gold and sailed back. But it was a tin of SpaghettiOs that conquered the great Aztec empire.

Moving north to North America we see the Native American civilizations that had been touched by Him. The most glaring evidence of His influence is the aspen tree. This tree's name was derived from the Ojibwa (aka Chippewa) term *Aspe* meaning "tree of gods that gives noodles, grows straight and tall, and rustles in the wind like the Noodly Appendages of the Great Flying One" (a minor side note; The Ojibwa were very good at shortening phrases into simple words). The truth provided by this tree of gods is self-evident in that the aspen has an inner bark that can be removed, cut into strips, and boiled into an edible noodly dish. This was very good when served with pemmican balls made of venison. This is very close to spaghetti and meatballs. While some scholars claim it was convergent Evolution, we know it was designed by the FSM. The early colonial culture was inspired by the gifts the FSM gave, including the gift of pasta. This is clearly expressed in the children's song lyric of "Yankee Doodle stuck a feather in his hat and called it macaroni." "Macaroni" . . . a simple coincidental rhyming word? I think not! It is historical fact. The revolutionary Charles Kraft started supplying the colonists with boxes of Kraft macaroni and cheese to spite the English, who were insisting everyone eat biscuits and jam. The use of macaroni was a way for early colonists to thumb their noses at King George through their dinner plates. The Flying Spaghetti Monster left his mark on Native American culture and helped the American Revolution strike a blow for democracy against tyranny. We now can move to another English colony, Australia.

Australia is a relatively newly discovered continent. It was left untouched by Europeans until very recently in human history. The clearest example of the guiding Noodly Appendage of the FSM is the kangaroo. These spry marsupials have witnessed the Great One and are working their way toward enlightenment. The little joeys realize that to fly like the FSM is the first step to godliness. So the joeys jump, trying to remain airborne for as long as possible in an attempt at flying. They spend their days meditatively trying to jump high enough to become airborne and fly like the great one. A group of older transcendental kangaroos (and one tigger, a catlike creature with tops made of rubber and bottoms of springs) have accomplished this and meditatively levitated through the air like the FSM. This meditative spell was promptly broken by the arrival of Japanese tourists snapping pictures of flying kangaroos led by a tigger. To reward the kangaroos for their faith the FSM arranged for the tourists to be eaten by Godzilla upon returning to Japan. The unintended consequence was that it also ruined their film, so the photo evidence of flying kangaroos being led by a tigger is lost to humanity. Otherwise there is only minor circumstantial evidence of His work in Australia. Most notable among this evidence is that the trees in the fairly lifeless outback are often referred to singularly as a "stringy bark," implying they pop up like the FSM flying upside down, which incidentally is why Australia is called "down under."

While Australia is replete with circumstantial evidence of the FSM, you need only travel to the north to discover evidence of a more concrete nature. China has the oldest fossilized noodles in the world. The archaeological community discovered an upturned bowl of noodles that had been fossilized over the last four thousand years, making them the oldest noodles in the world. There were reports of seven bowls of fossilized noodles dating back to 8000 B.C.E. discovered in the southern Yangtze Province, but those were looted and served as "extra crunchy fried noodles" to the lunch crowd at City Wok in South Park, Colorado, for $3.95 plus tax. Any noodles left over were devoured by a corpulent nine-year-old boy of foul demeanor and temperament. Thus, the validity of this finding cannot be verified. This is just another case of how looting of antiquities causes their loss to the scientific community as a whole. Other evidence in Asia is the variations of noodles available. One can find short crisp noodles served as chow mein noodles in China, pad thai noodles in Thailand, and Ramen noodles in Japan, just to name a few. So noodles are an important part of the diet of Asia. In contrast, we will proceed to the last continent, Antarctica.

Antarctica, the cursed, is the continent that is the Pastafarian equivalent to Christianity's Hell. The Beer Volcano froze over millennia ago, the strippers wear big bulky parkas and snow pants, and the place is covered in ice and snow. The only native inhabitants are the ones cursed by Him. He has cast out those who have forsaken Him, the penguins. The short stout penguins are the direct descendants of the original midget. The midget got mad at the FSM for making him short and out of anger cursed the Great One loudly and profanely. In retaliation, the vengeful FSM cast the reject to the coldest part of the world, and morphed the degenerate into a penguin. The penguin is the opposite of all that is godly. It has wings, but cannot fly. It has flippers instead of hands, so is unable to pick up noodles. It eats naught but fish, which makes nasty fishy meatballs. He created a land that is incapable of growing anything worthy of pasta creation; krill, the only thing the penguins have to make noodles from, tastes disgusting. Thus Antarctica is the land of rejected creations. Learning from this mistake, the next thing He made after the midget was a dwarf, which turned out pretty hilarious when it got drunk from the volcano and started simultaneously swearing at and hitting on the strippers. So the FSM kept dwarfs as an amusing distraction. He was so distracted he forgot the next thing on His to-do list, "make penguin-eating sharks."

So we can see by the preponderance of evidence that it is beyond a shadow of a doubt that the Great Flying Spaghetti Monster created everything in the world and has influenced Evolution throughout all of history. It has been shown that His Noodly Appendage has touched every continent and every civilization around the globe. This evidence has been carefully cataloged by the scribes assigned to the great Pirate sailing vessels as they journey around the world gathering archaeological evidence of the Great One. The only continent they avoid is Antarctica, and that is because they know not to go there; Shackleton brought back records of what the ungrateful penguins tried to do to him and his crew when they were stranded there. This evidence spans the globe, made manifest in the chow mein noodles of China, the aspen noodles of Nebraska, the flying kangaroos of Australia, and the great megaghetti boats of the ancient Phoenicians. This should settle all debates over the influence of the Flying Spaghetti Monster.

FSM Theologebra

CHURCH OF THE FLYING SPAGHETTI MONSTER: ALGEBRA

Alexander Gross

Profound science uses mathematics to prove theories. This paper introduces fundamental algebra and Boolean logic into theology to prove that the Flying Spaghetti Monster is the one and only god. The perspective shown here makes any other philosophy senseless and undesirable. Actually, it has the potential to negate even itself—dear God, what have I done?

Before starting to prove god, it is necessary to extend Boolean logic with a few new operators:

The then-and-only-then operator:	&&
The not-or-never operator:	##
The so-it-is term:	Υ

These three symbols are defined by the following relations, where x is an arbitrary variable of any dimension:

$$\partial x/\partial\&\& + \partial x/\partial\#\# = \&\& \times \#\# = \#\# \times \&\& = \Upsilon$$

Additionally, some religiously important symbols have to be declared:

The god operator:	👽
The enlightenment constant:	☦
The religion symbol:	Я
The faith symbol:	†

Now let the set of all major religions be defined as Я = {ø, ✍, 👽, †, ☪, ‡}, where ø stands for Atheism, ✍ for Flying Spaghetti Monster Church, 👽 for Buddhism, † for Christianity, ☪ for Islam, and ‡ for Hinduism.

Simple vector algebra helps define the logical religion equations where $n < \infty$, $n \in N$:

$$\varnothing = \#\# \cdot 👽$$
$$\text{≈} = n + (1 \cdot 👽)$$
$$👁 = ☥$$
$$† = 1 \cdot 👽$$
$$☾ = (\&\& \cdot 👽)$$
$$‡ = (n + n^2) \cdot 👽$$

The interpretation of *n* is not as easy as one may expect. It represents the amount of believed influence of god in everyday life. In Hinduism, two terms containing *n* are present because of the great number of gods in which they believe. The FSM Church has one *n* factor because its god is still alive. The other elements of Я either have a dead messiah or no god at all.

As you may have noticed, a god difference Δ 👽 ("delta god") is present, which can of course be calculated by summation of all god factors:

$$\Delta 👽 = \#\# + 1 + 0 + 1 + \&\& + n + n^2$$
$$\Delta 👽 = n^2 + n + 2$$

This outstanding quadratic equation will be solved later in this paper.

In general, the faith symbol is defined to be the sum of god's influence on earth:

$$† = \int n \, dn$$
$$† = \tfrac{1}{2} \cdot n^2 \qquad \dots \text{Conservation of faith}$$

LEMMA: All elements of Я show a profound *conservation of faith*. This is similar to the *conservation of energy* in physics.

Sometimes, someone ministers an ecumenical church service. In this case, the god difference is zero. A little historical excursus leads us to Ecumenes, who was the first to prove this important equation. Ecumenes fulfilled all criteria of a human being except the criterion of existence. What a pity. This important equation also allows solving the quadratic equation mentioned earlier:

$$\Delta \cdot 👽 = 0 \qquad \text{... 1st principle of Ecumenes}$$
$$n^2 + n + 2 = 0$$
$$n = -\tfrac{1}{2} \cdot \sqrt{(\tfrac{1}{4} - 2)}$$
$$n = -\tfrac{1}{2} \cdot \sqrt{(-7 \cdot \tfrac{1}{4})}$$
$$n = -\tfrac{1}{2} \cdot i \cdot \sqrt{(7 \cdot \tfrac{1}{4})}$$
$$n = -0.66i \qquad \text{... 2nd principle of Ecumenes}$$

LEMMA: Solving the *first principle of Ecumenes* leads to introducing the complex numbers into FSM Theologebra.

The next issue illustrates how useful mathematical methods applied to nonalgebraic subjects can be. In general, the gradient results in the direction of a multidimensional structure. Assuming that god is a multidimensional structure, the *divergence* of god, written $\nabla \cdot 👽$, represents *god's will*. Applying our extended Boolean structure on the Nabla symbol, we can define it as the derivation after && (then-and-only-then) and ## (not-or-never) and insert the god operator:

$$\nabla = (\partial/\partial \&\&, \partial/\partial \#\#)^T$$
$$\nabla \cdot 👽 = \partial 👽/\partial \&\& + \partial 👽/\partial \#\# \qquad /\partial x/\partial \&\& + \partial x/\partial \#\# = \&\& \times \#\# = \Upsilon$$
$$\nabla \cdot 👽 = \&\& \times \#\# = \Upsilon \qquad \text{/in words: "God's will, so it is."}$$

A different philosophical approach to this topic brings us closer to the question: "What does God really want?" This is very easy to answer. God wants faith to arise with greater influence and he wants himself to arise with greater influence. This results in a second equation for god's will:

$$\nabla \cdot 👽 = \partial \dagger/\partial n + \partial 👽/\partial n \qquad \text{/ insert the } \textit{conservation of faith}$$
$$\nabla \cdot 👽 = \partial(\tfrac{1}{2} \cdot n^2)/\partial n + \partial 👽/\partial n \qquad \text{/ solve the derivatives}$$
$$\nabla \cdot 👽 = n + (1 \cdot 👽) \qquad \text{/ insert the 2nd principle of Ecumenes}$$
$$\nabla \cdot 👽 = -0.66i + (1 \cdot 👽) \qquad /\text{☙} = -0.66i + (1 \cdot 👽) = n + (1 \cdot 👽)$$
$$\nabla \cdot 👽 = \text{☙}$$

In words: "God's will is the Church of the Flying Spaghetti God."

Inserting this result into the earlier result for god's will implies

$$\nabla \, \text{👽} \; = \; \&\& \times \; \#\# \; = \; \text{🌀}$$
$$\text{🌀} \; = \; \text{𝛶}$$

Spoken: "Church of the Flying Spaghetti God—so it is."

Pirates and Faith
Alexis Drummond

It has been a sad fact to Pastafarians globally that Piracy is on the decline. This displeases our Noodly Lord, the Flying Spaghetti Monster, and He has shown His discontent by showering us with more and more natural disasters. This past year alone shows just how much we have incurred His wrath, from tsunamis and hurricanes and earthquakes, not to mention the ever-worrisome dilemma of global warming. But to those who are not well-versed in FSMism, it must seem a puzzle why our merciful and great Noodly Lord should choose Pirates as His shepherds.

To answer this question, we must look back to days when these noble swashbucklers roamed the high seas. Pirates were a superstitious bunch, and tales abound as to the creatures they encountered. One famous example is the myth that upon encountering manatees, Pirates mistook them to be mermaids. In reality our holy texts show undeniable evidence that mermaids are in fact real, but the Flying Spaghetti Monster, in His infinite Noodly wisdom, has hidden them from us to express His growing ire. But I digress.

More important, one myth made especially famous by *Twenty Thousand Leagues under the Sea* is maritime struggles with a giant squid. It is easy enough to take these claims at face value, but when one probes deeper some things become suspect. For instance, for decades the only evidence science has been able to offer are dead specimens. Why is it, all of a sudden after such a long search, that one was finally "discovered" alive? And what is a squid after all but a creature with many tentacles and giant eyes?

The truth, we Pastafarians know, is that this first myth of a giant squid was the Flying Spaghetti Monster revealing Himself unto His Chosen People. They were true believers in the power He held and of His Noodly Might, and so He granted them the rare and awesome opportunity of an audience. It has been speculated by many FSMist scholars that the first mention of an angry squid attacking a ship was in fact the Flying Spaghetti Monster hugging the ship for its faithfulness, and a nearby naval vessel, which had been hoping to arrest these pious souls, mistook our Noodly Lord's loving embrace for a cruel sea monster rather than the good and gracious Flying Spaghetti Monster that He is.

As for this evidence allegedly found by scientists, we are of the belief that the Flying Spaghetti Monster created the one living example of a giant squid as a test to see who was a true believer. For those without faith, or whose faith was weak, the squid confirmed these myths. For those of us who wholeheartedly believe in the Flying Spaghetti Monster, we knew that this was merely a false messiah with nothing but hollow promises and an unusual smell. It is this latter group who shall be truly rewarded for understanding that the Noodly Lord can create weird creatures like giant squids just as easily as He can plant "evidence" of a fossil record dating back what appears to be several thousand years, as well as make them seemingly link together in a systematic Evolutionary process. All dead specimens and infant specimens found of the giant squid are indeed bits of His Noodly Appendage that He has doffed, and by the miracle of Him they formed a creature similar to His shape, though nowhere near His perfection and beauty.

Now that we understand the importance of Pirates, we must turn to the dilemma of the decreased number of them in this world. True, there are many Internet Pirates bootlegging music and movies, but the overwhelming majority of them do not garb themselves in the regalia mandated by such a noble title. While we FSMists cannot condone any illegality on the behalf of these individuals, we would like to take this opportunity to encourage any who partake in these activities to find appropriate attire suitable for their profession.

In conclusion, Pirates are an essential part not only of our own faith, but of the welfare of our entire planet. Any devout Pastafarian ought to don piratical regalia on all religious holidays, as well as when preaching the Good Word to those who have not yet discovered the saving grace of the Flying Spaghetti Monster. After looking at this overwhelming evidence and being touched by His Noodly Appendage, I can't imagine who wouldn't say "a Pirate's life for me."

Evidence of the Baker
J. R. Blackwell

If we were to walk along the beach together, holding hands, and were to find at our feet a German chocolate cake, we would undoubtedly be surprised. Our shock at finding this seductive pastry results from the inborn knowledge that cake does not rise from the sands unbidden. A cake must have a baker. We understand that cakes do not simply appear randomly out of the void because of their form and complexity; if the frosting were removed, or the butter replaced with tuna salad, what we would have before us would not be the delicious concoction that we call cake. It would be burned, unfrosted tuna, and that would be disappointing. There had to be a Baker for our cake, and further, since it is a glistening, moist German chocolate cake, there must also be Germans.

For we all also know that, like cake, chocolate is not naturally occurring. Chocolate must be created by Germans, people who have alchemic power over the raw substance of cacao, thus to make it into the divine element we know as chocolate. The process of making chocolate is a mystical one, as any process that creates such a delicious product must undoubtedly be. The creators of chocolate are almost as complex as the chocolate itself, and tracing this line of logic, we begin to comprehend that chocolate makers (Germans) must also have a Baker. The majestic nature of chocolate clearly points to a mystical origin, and since the world is full of majesty, we suddenly understand that this Baker must also be a source of great spiritual power as well.

This world, which is infinitely more complex than cake, even if the cake is both German and chocolate, cannot occur out of chance: It must have a divine Baker. There are levels of form and purpose that will not rise without the intervention of a Baker, and the world is full of such mixed and layered forms. The most striking of these forms is that of a Pirate.

Nothing but the divine could have created such a glorious creature as the Pirate, let alone a ship full of Pirates! Pirates could only have been created by a divine Baker who, with His wisdom, applied levels of logic and organization to the completed life of all existence. A Pirate is made up of several distinct elements: his love for the sea, his fanciful attire, his endless search for booty, and his parrot. His love of the sea is complex, for, as he loves the lady of the sea, breaking her maidenhead with each thrust of his prow, he also scorns her, as she brings him storms and danger. A Pirate has fanciful costume; sashes and golden rings that could not have emerged from the void, but have a form and function made specifically for the body of the Pirate. His lustful search for booty borders on an obsession, an endless quest for the hidden island that rumors say contains a cursed treasure. It seems contradictory that a Pirate would search for cursed treasure, but that in itself is evidence of the divine plan of our Baker.

Even the parrot that sits perched on the Pirate's shoulder is masterfully formed, a creature able to mimic the Pirate's own words, lending an ominous weight to their meaning. Such a bird could not have been created from a process by which elements available in the primordial stew of a young earth experienced passing electrical currents that stimulated them to form a variety of molecules, including a self-replicating molecule, which, over time, produced varieties that competed with one another for resources, becoming ever more complex through competition and mutation, some of which developed strategies involving cooperation for an advantage in the replication process, an advantage that produced an interactive whole that could have developed limbs for movement, light-sensitive cells that eventually became eyes, and bright colorful feathers that would be used to attract mates and thus continue the process of replication originated in those basic self-replicating molecules of the primordial stew. *No!* That explanation is far too complex to be accurate, and moreover, I don't understand it, so it must be wrong.

What I do understand is cake. Cake, especially German chocolate cake, is scrumptious and was made by a Baker. The theory of science speculates that at the creation of things, there was a Big Bang. Could we not see this as a Big Baking? What of the Baker? Who, at the beginning of time, baked all things, completed the mixing, and rolled out the world, giving it a warm center and a crispy crust? Who was this Baker, this elemental divinity who created the world? Our only explanation for this Baker is the Flying Spaghetti Monster, the creature that mystically baked the world into being. Holy men with the gift of sight are able to discern the teachings of the Flying Spaghetti Monster. These holy men are good guys, not above lending a ten-spot or buying a guy a beer. To say that they are wrong, that what they preach is not complete fact, is to say that they are evil liars, which I will not stand by and listen to you say about our holy men.

Scientists claim that the creation of the earth was something involving math or chemicals. I find math and the physical sciences to be irritating, and those scientists, none of whom have ever lent me a ten-spot, are stuck-up jerks who are blind to the truth of the Flying Spaghetti Monster. How many elephants had to die to make their ivory towers? Jerks.

Evidence of a Holy Baker is in our world, in cake and in chocolate. Scientists tell us that the world was a stew, when I think it is clearly a layered cake. They have the stew idea, and I have a theory that stands by cake. Who but the divine, who was actually there, could say which one of us is right? Cakes are made by mortal bakers, chocolate is divinely mixed by Germans, and Pirates are inexplicably complex. All these factors lead us to the conclusion that our world was created by the Flying Spaghetti Monster, who, in His wisdom, baked us all.

Piracy as a Preventor of Tropical Cyclones

Jacob D. Haqq-Misra

DEPARTMENT OF METEOROLOGY

PENNSYLVANIA STATE UNIVERSITY

Michael B. Larson

DEPARTMENT OF PHYSICS AND ASTRONOMY

UNIVERSITY OF WYOMING

ABSTRACT

Recent hurricane seasons have been characterized by intense and frequent tropical cyclones. One contributor is the increased sea-surface temperature, which is caused by decreased upwelling of cold deep-ocean water. We demonstrate that decreased Pirate activity results in less upwelling. This suggests that the only viable solution to intense tropical cyclones is to increase Pirate activity.

INTRODUCTION

The destructiveness of the 2004 and 2005 hurricane seasons has heightened public and scientific awareness of the possible long-term consequences of global warming. Although the link between hurricane strength and global warming remains speculative, recent work has shown that hurricanes have intensified over the past thirty years (Emmanuel, 2005), with an increase in the number of category 4 and 5 hurricanes and a decrease in those classified as categories 1 and 2. Emmanuel (1987) argued that hurricane intensity is a function of the sea surface temperature (SST) which, of course, increases as the earth warms. But other factors are important as well. Lighthill et al. (1994) pointed out that while a lower SST limit of 26°C is required for tropical cyclone formation, several other key factors contribute to formation and intensity.

The increase in global average temperature is well correlated with a decrease in global Pirate population, as evident in Figure 1 (Henderson 2006).

Figure 1

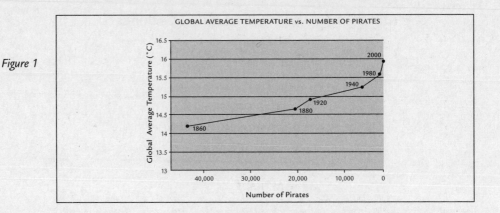

PIRACY AND UPWELLING

Piracy decreases the average SST by inducing upwelling of cold deep-ocean water. Various Pirate activities contribute to upwelling. These include involuntary crew resignation, intervessel interactions, and acoustically transmitted oscillations (Bligh, 1789; Stevenson, 1883).

Involuntary crew resignation (ICR, aka "walking the plank") involves a Pirate or captive being forcibly ejected from a vessel at sea. This results in upwelling from displacement of water by the ejectee (Archimedes, c. 250 B.C.E.).

Intervessel interactions (IVI, aka "sea combat") consists of transmission of projectiles between vessels, resulting in destruction or boarding. Upwelling is caused by scattered projectiles and by sinking of vessel elements.

Acoustically transmitted oscillations (ATO, aka "sea shanties") were originally intended to boost morale of rowing Pirates. They have assumed ritual functions with the ascent of external power supplies. ATOs produce upwelling by disturbing the sea surface. This increases motion of large biological entities ("fish" or "whales"), producing displacement.

MODEL RESULTS

We have modeled Pirate-induced upwelling using the PARROT (Piratic Activity Realization Rate of Oceanic Tendencies) oceanic circulation

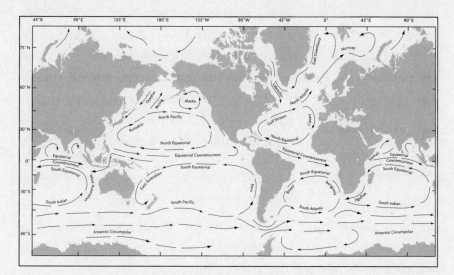

Figure 2a

model (Haqq-Misra et al., 2006). This model has 0.5° resolution and accurately reproduces present-day ocean currents (Figure 2a).

We simulated normalized Pirate-induced upwelling (in upwelling Pirate units, or upu) over the three upwelling categories described above. An ICR event produces 1 upu. IVIs produce a variable number of upu. We used a Maxwellian with an average of 1,000 upu. It should be noted that IVI events can produce multiple ICRs. ATO produces continuous

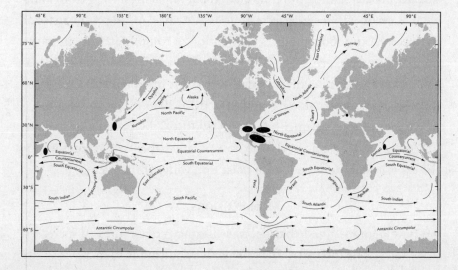

Figure 2b

upwelling, based on the local Pirate density and oceanic biotic activity. The world average ATO is about 0.5 upu/day.

We averaged Pirate activity from 1605 to 2005 for each ocean grid cell. While recent Pirate activity is weak and concentrated off the Somali coast (BBC, 2005), historically Piracy has been concentrated in the Caribbean (Bruckheimer, 2003). This is consistent with our model results, which produce significant Pirate-induced upwelling in the Atlantic basin (Figure 2b).

DISCUSSION

We have demonstrated that Pirate activity produces upwelling. It is thus obvious that a decreasing Pirate population will result in less oceanic upwelling, especially in the Atlantic basin.

As evidenced by the 2004 and 2005 hurricane seasons, decreased upwelling results in increased SSTs and more intense tropical cyclones. Our PARROT model predicts that if the downward trend in Piracy continues, tropical cyclones will intensify. The hurricane season may also lengthen due to increased SST.

PREDICTIONS AND EXPERIMENT

The PARROT model has not been experimentally verified. Therefore, we have predicted the upwelling and global impact resulting from a single ICR event. While the effects of an ICR event depend on the mass of the ejectee, our model predicts a reduction of roughly 10 percent in the number of named tropical storms in the Atlantic basin in the 2006 season as a result of a relatively small ICR event off the northern Puerto Rican coast between March 9 and March 13, 2006.

We intend to experimentally verify PARROT by producing such an ICR event. At least one of the authors of this paper will be present for the experiment, to measure the exact upu value of the event.

CONCLUSIONS

We have demonstrated that decreased Piracy contributes to increased tropical cyclone intensity. The only viable solution is to increase Pirate activity, especially in the Atlantic basin. We suggest that ICRs and ATO are preferable to IVIs, because they offer finer control of upwelling effects.

ACKNOWLEDGMENTS

We thank the Flying Spaghetti Monster for inspiring this work and Robert Henderson for advocating Piracy to fight global climate change.

REFERENCES

Archimedes (of Syracuse). c. 250 B.C.E. *On Floating Bodies.* Syracuse, Greece.

Bligh, W. 1789. *Log of the H.M.S. Bounty.* Royal Navy, London, UK.

British Broadcasting Corporation. Nov. 25, 2005. "US Firm to Fight Somali Pirates." London, UK.

Bruckheimer, J. 2003. *Pirates of the Caribbean.* Disney Enterprises, Orlando, Fla., USA.

Emanuel, K. A. 1987. "The Dependence of Hurricane Intensity on Climate." *Nature,* 326, 483–485.

———. 2005. "Increasing Destructiveness of Tropical Cyclones over the Past Thirty Years." *Nature,* 436, 686–688.

Haqq-Misra, J. D., et al. 2006. *A Predictive Ocean Circulation Model.* In press.

Henderson, R. 2006. *The Gospel of the Flying Spaghetti Monster.* Villard, New York.

Lighthill, J., et al. 1994. "Tropical Cyclones and Global Climate Change." *BAMS,* 75, 2147–2157.

Stevenson, R. L. 1883. *Treasure Island.* Cassell & Co., London, UK.

Life, Kolgoromov Complexity, and Delicious Spaghetti
Nick Moran

To begin, let us look at the forms of life we can see on this planet. They all exhibit a certain degree of complexity that is not found in nonliving matter. A dog is much more complex than a rock. To express this, we can use the concept of Kolgoromov complexity. Living things possess high Kolgoromov complexity, because their DNA is decidedly uncompressible. As an example, consider the string of bits 10101010. This string has very low Kolgoromov complexity because it can be compressed to "write 10 four times." On the other hand, the string 0100101 is uncompressible in the same sense that DNA is. It has very high Kolgoromov complexity. That string was generated by me tapping the "0" and "1" keys on my keyboard.

If I had a keyboard with only ACGT, I could similarly write random DNA. If we put that DNA into a cell, and tried to make a living organism out of it, I very much doubt we would get anything living, much less good at living. Therefore, the uncompressible complexity we observe in living things is also nonrandom. It has been created for a purpose: the purpose of building living things.

So, if the DNA has been created, then there must be a creator. Some choose to posit the Christian God, other choose intelligent aliens with amazing technology. The problem is that both of these choices also must have extremely high Kolgoromov complexity. My chances of randomly hammering out the code to a divine being on my four-key keyboard are even less than that of coming up with a living animal. These are really just restatements of the same problem; we still don't know where the complexity came from. We could posit an endless string of gods each of whom created the one before it, thus accounting for the extremely high complexity of a god. However, this string just results in higher and higher degrees of complexity and gets us nowhere. What we need is a way to get high complexity from low complexity.

If you'll indulge me a brief tangent, I would like to discuss the properties of spaghetti. Imagine a box of uncooked spaghetti. It's essentially a series of straight lines. A box of two hundred pieces of spaghetti has very low Kolgoromov complexity. You could easily compress the data contained in those two hundred pieces. Now imagine a plate of cooked spaghetti, complete with sauce and, if you like, meatballs. Imagine the process of untangling this mass. It would take hours to take each individual piece of spaghetti, clean off the sauce, and put it in its own separate place and pick out the meatballs. This plate of spaghetti, all tangled up and covered with delicious sauce has very high complexity. Spaghetti has the astounding property of being able to go from very low to very high complexity.

Now, let's return to our search for a creator. Clearly gods and superintelligent aliens don't help us in our problem. A spaghetti god, however, could. It is reasonable that something of low complexity might come into existence on its own. We don't look at a rock in the woods and feel the need for a designer. So, low-complexity, uncooked spaghetti does not require a creator, it is quite capable of arising through random, natural processes. Then, when cooked via the infusion of energy, it can come to have a high complexity. Consider the difference between uncooked and slightly cooked spaghetti. Slightly cooked spaghetti has slightly higher complexity than uncooked. There is a continuous spectrum from low to high as the spaghetti is cooked. The more the spaghetti is cooked, the more energy has been infused. In order to create a Flying Spaghetti Monster capable of creating life, which would have an extremely high level of complexity, we would need an extremely high amount of energy to do the cooking.

There is only one place where we might find the required amount of energy: the universe immediately following the Big Bang. Temperatures of 100 billion degrees Kelvin would certainly be sufficient to generate the high Kolgoromov complexity of spaghetti with the power to create life.

Thus, we have found a solution to the question of where the Kolgoromov complexity of life comes from. Uncooked spaghetti arose naturally (quite possibly because of its low Kolgoromov complexity) during the first instants of the universe. It was then cooked by the extremely high temperatures, causing it to rapidly gain complexity to the point of being able to create life. Further increases in complexity granted it the ability to fly, and monster status.

There will likely be some neo-Darwinian, Ivy League, science elitist who will come up with some other object that can rise in complexity when cooked. In order to prove that the true form of the creator is that of a Flying Spaghetti Monster, I will employ a version of the famed cosmological argument:

1. You don't need a reason to enjoy spaghetti.
2. Everything (else) has a cause.
3. Nothing can cause itself.
4. Everything is caused by another thing.
5. A causal chain cannot be of infinite length.
6. There must be a first cause.
7. The first cause had no cause.
8. Spaghetti is the only thing that can have no cause, thus must be the first cause.

QED, bitches.

A Twenty-first-Century Ontological Argument
Kevin Heinright

A classic argument for the existence of god is known as the ontological argument (henceforth OA). This argument was developed by Saint Anselm in the eleventh century, but has been greatly improved upon in the ensuing years. The argument, in a nutshell, is that a perfect being must necessarily exist. It is part of the very nature of a perfect being to be real—all beings that do not exist are by definition imperfect. This is because it is better to exist than to not exist (that is, to exist brings you closer to perfection). So if we can merely conceive of a perfect being, then it must, on pain of contradiction, be real.

In a popular formulation of the OA, we are asked to imagine a being of which no greater can be conceived. One might motivate this process by creating a list of perfections. Reasonably, such a list would include omnipotence, omniscience, benevolence, being the creator of all of reality, and so on. We are then asked to compare this list with one in which the characteristic of "actual existence" has been added. Obviously the second list describes a more perfect being. It is clear then that the first list was not a description of a being *of which no greater can be conceived.* No matter what characteristics we have imagined, actual existence would be an improvement. Hence whatever characteristics we attribute to our perfect being, existence must be one of them.

While there have been many criticisms of the OA, from Kantian metaphysics to modern quantificational logic, we believe all such challenges can be answered. However, we do not have time to review the nuances of this debate. For more detailed information, please see http://plato.stanford.edu/entries/ontological-arguments/.

Traditionally it has been argued (to be frank, it has generally only been assumed) that the necessarily existent perfect being fits comfortably into the Judeo-Christian mold. Now surely any perfect being has the characteristics listed above: it is omnipotent, omniscient, benevolent, and the creator of all reality. Here we have no quarrel with tradition. However, we will soon see that there are several other characteristics that have been overlooked (or suppressed) by philosophers and theologians during the last millennium. We propose that a careful review of the reasoning behind the OA will indicate that rather than the god of the Judeo-Christian tradition, the OA indicates the existence of a mass of starchy substance capable of gravity resistance. Such a being must necessarily be, and so all denials of its existence involve blatant logical contradiction.

We will begin our argument with an experience most people can share. When a young person moves away from home and goes to college, he finds himself confronted for the first time with the task of providing himself with the necessities of life. For many a college freshman, this proves a nearly unsurmountable task. While one can survive without paying the gas, electric, and phone bills, all living things require sustenance in order to continue to live. And what is the staple diet of the impoverished student? Ramen noodles, macaroni and cheese, and spaghetti. But it is not merely college students in first-world nations who subsist on this food. The staple diet of a large portion of humanity is starchy noodles. The unique properties of this foodstuff make it the most popular form of subsistence in all of recorded history. Noodles are high in caloric content, they are nutritious, and they are simple and easy to produce. Clearly, then, noodles are an objectively superior food. Indeed, noodles are the perfect food.

We will demonstrate that our perfect being must be made of the most perfect food. Before we continue, however, a potentially serious objection must be met.

Some will argue that because rice is a staple diet of so many people in the world, it must be the more perfect food. On the contrary, we argue that rice is a profoundly evil form of sustenance. The corrupting nature of rice should be evident to anyone who has taken seriously the twentieth-century battles against the evils of communism. This small, deceptive grain has provided the fuel for millions of communist soldiers, communist spies, and communist infiltrators. What countries remain communist in the twenty-first century? China, Vietnam, and Korea come to mind immediately. Now, what food is most commonly associated with these nations? Certainly not spaghetti! The case against rice should be immediately clear. (As a side note, this result should be of more than casual philosophical interest. A central part of modern struggles against tyranny should involve changing the eating habits of those living under oppressive regimes.)

Now, why must a perfect being be composed of the perfect food? The argument is surprisingly straightforward. Since food is necessary for life, and life is more perfect than nonlife, food is the fundamental substance, or substratum, of all living things. All living things are made of food. The perfect being exists, and because it is a being (rather than a nonbeing, such as a very small rock), it is necessarily alive. But of what shall our most perfect being be made? The most perfect food. Hence, the perfect being is made of some kind of pasta.

Another perfection is gravity resistance. Modern science holds that gravity is a "weak" force. However, this is in clear contradiction to the evidence. Anyone who has ever climbed a flight of stairs, fallen from a great height, or hiked up a mountain can attest that gravity is a strong force indeed. The scientific elites tell us otherwise, but the contradictions in modern physics are evident to even the most casual observer. If gravity were a weak force, then surely the rotation of the earth would cast us all into space. Does electromagnetism keep Mount Everest in its place? Even a child can see the contradictions here. Only someone with an overabundance of education could deny the evidence of their senses in such an absurd way. Contrary to modern physics (which is corrupted by naturalism, Evolutionism, and antipastaism), gravity is the strongest force in the universe. Surely, then, a perfect being is capable of resisting the greatest force in His creation. Hence, our perfect being is capable of gravity resistance (that is, flight).

We hope this essay enables the reader to see the rational necessity of belief in the Flying Spaghetti Monster.

The truths of this world are not difficult to find, and much effort (and money!) could be saved if we were willing to accept the futility and error of so-called "scientific" reasoning and spend our time in careful contemplation of His Noodly Greatness.

Arghh.

Note: The arguments, which demonstrate that a perfect being would require mortals to dress as Pirates, are too obvious to merit inclusion in this essay. This derivation is left for the reader.

On the matter of spheres of meaty substance in the pasta matrix, we remain agnostic. One must not extend one's reasoning beyond what is available in terms of first principles and evidence. Some room must be left for faith.

Mathematical Proof of the FSM
James Hofer

Proof of the Flying Spaghetti Monster's existence:

Given:

  The Flying Spaghetti Monster is frequently represented as FSM.

  Existence is the opposite of nonexistence, or therefore not Null.

  Null is frequently represented as 0.

  We will use $<>$ to show nonequivalence.

Therefore to prove that the Flying Spaghetti Monster exists, we must prove that:

  $FSM <> 0$

In physics, force is equal to mass time acceleration, or $F = MA$. Bobby Henderson is a physics graduate, so we can substitute this into the above equation, giving us:

  $(MA)SM <> 0$
  $MASM <> 0$

MASM is the microsoft assembler, which most definitely exists, therefore $MASM <> 0$. Microsoft is one of the most successful businesses in history, undoubtedly as a result of their secret ties to the Flying Spaghetti Monster.

Einstein's equation $E = MC^2$ can also be substituted into the above equation.

  $E = MC^2 \rightarrow M = E/C^2 = E/(CC)$
  $FS(E/CC) <> 0$
  $FSE/CC <> 0$

It's obvious that both the FCC and the SEC exist—just ask Howard Stern and Martha Stewart—government agencies that seek to control things, much like the Noodly Master. What most people don't know is that FSE/CC is Federation of Swaziland Employers and Chamber of Commerce. The king of Swaziland recently picked a new wife by having thirty thousand women walk topless in front of him. This is obviously because he is a devout follower of the Flying Spaghetti Monster and, knowing about the Stripper Factory in Heaven, wanted to create Heaven on earth.

Thus, since we have shown that MASM, FCC, SEC, and FSE/CC all exist, we have proven that FSM <> 0 and the Flying Spaghetti Monster exists.

A Corporate Proof of the Flying Spaghetti Monster
Scott Stoddard

I just celebrated my one-year anniversary with my current employer. Actually, I completely forgot, but they did not. I received a very nice, but god-awful useless, sterling-silver key chain with the company logo. It's nice to be appreciated. It also got me thinking.

If everything on earth is God's handiwork, then He really is the worst kind of micromanager. I don't want to believe that.

Let's assume that God exists. Can't prove it. Can't disprove it. Doesn't hurt to think that there is an all powerful deity with a corner office somewhere out there in the cosmos.

Now, THE UNIVERSE is a pretty big place. It probably isn't a privately held company. I'd be willing to bet that THE UNIVERSE incorporated years ago. In a business model, God would be the CEO.

That would make God accountable to the Board of Directors of THE UNIVERSE, INC.

Who makes up this board? What are their terms of office? And for that matter, would we, as residents of THE EARTH, be considered stockholders or employees of the corporation? Let's assume employees. I know I've never received any dividends or letters of proxy.

I think that everyone would agree that THE EARTH is a dangerous place. Humanity is continually trying to destroy itself. Throw in a bitchy Mother Nature with her tsunamis, earthquakes, and hurricanes, and you have what any businessman would call a high-risk venture.

So now, the main question is this:

Would God, the CEO of THE UNIVERSE, INC., take a hands-on approach to the creation and management of THE EARTH?

I think not.

God, being the smart CEO we all know he is, would most likely have handed the project off to a Vice President for Strategic Development of THE UNIVERSE, INC. This would, of course, limit God's liability to the Board of Directors of THE UNIVERSE, INC.

In turn the VP, not wanting to be immersed in a corporate scandal should anything go wrong, probably had Accounting form a shell corporation called THE EARTH, INC., and promoted some hot-shot middle manager to oversee the whole thing. I believe that the Flying Spaghetti Monster is this manager.

The FSM, wanting to spread the wealth, brings over some of his buddies, who might be great guys to go drinking with, but who really aren't suited for managing an entire planet. This would explain famine, disease, suffering, and stupidity—corporate cronyism at its worst.

Don't you think this theory of Intelligent Design just fits together a little more soundly than God Himself creating THE EARTH, INC.?

If we make it to another millennium without folding, do we all get silver key chains?

A Final Note from Bobby Henderson and His Staff

D EAR NEWLY CONVERTED READER,

I think it's safe to say that FSMism is not only a ground-breaking religion but the only one supported by hard science. This makes it probably the most unquestionably true theory ever put forth in the history of humankind. And yet we find doubters and naysayers galore, mostly in the form of Evolutionists, ID supporters, and members of other religions. But we live in America, a country founded on, among other things, the idea of religious freedom. We have laws to protect people against religious persecution.

In spite of these laws, you may encounter people who disagree with your right to miss school or work every Friday, to wear an eye patch in public, to talk like a pirate, etc. Your first step should always be to tell these sceptics a little about our beliefs. They may simply convert to FSMism, in which case your problem is solved. But sometimes it's not that easy. If, after learning about our religion, people still refuse to allow you to express your constitutionally protected right of freedom of religion, then you should write a letter. If you're in school, write a letter to the principal, copying the superintendent of the school district, as well as your local chapter of the ACLU. If you're at work, write to your supervisor, copying the company's director of human resources—and, again, forward a copy to the ACLU. The important thing is not to sit back and let your rights be trampled on.

To those hardened Evolutionists, we would remind you that we're not saying Evolution couldn't have happened—only that it is most likely a process guided by His Noodly Appendage. We know that the FSM may be working behind the scenes to make Evolution look plausible. We also know that He might not be doing so. The Flying Spaghetti Monster works in mysterious ways, and He definitely messes with stuff all the time, though we know not why.

To the proponents of Intelligent Design, we offer you this olive branch: Pastafarians support your argument that *only* teaching Evolution in schools unfairly discriminates against those with creation beliefs. We know about your efforts to develop a wedge strategy, whereby you seek to keep the Bible out of the discussion for now, instead concentrating on establishing "scientific" evidence of a creator. Pastafarians see the wisdom of this approach, and we offer our own fork strategy, in which we argue for the inclusion of supernatural explanations in science—thus opening the door for FSMism to be taught one day. Quite simply, we are brothers in this effort.

Everyone knows that theories aren't the same as facts, and there is little doubt that alternative theories must be taught alongside more established ones. We've pointed to much evidence supporting His existence, certainly enough to get Pastafarianism included in the curriculum alongside Evolution and Intelligent Design. And when we turn our minds toward the world's great religions, we can admit that the other ones are pretty good, but ours is still the Best. Religion. Ever. Why not teach all the theories and let the kids decide?

We hope you've enjoyed our book. If not, we hope that you've at least learned something. If you didn't learn anything, it is our sincere wish that *The Gospel of the FSM* made you think. If you didn't even have a thought, then there's no doubt you're a Born-Again Christian, in which case we hope that you're able to keep off the crack long enough to get a vasectomy or have your tubes tied.

Okay, that last sentence was mean and I apologize. Pastafarians are a community of peaceful and open-minded worshippers, which means that anything we've said or done to offend people[1] was meant only in the spirit of promoting greater understanding and awareness. It has been said that the best sauce requires an occasional stir or two—wiser words have seldom been spoken—and so we have done our best to stir the waters of belief in the hopes of converting just a few more Pirates to His Noodly Goodness. RAmen.

BOBBY HENDERSON
Prophet

1 Including midgets, of course.

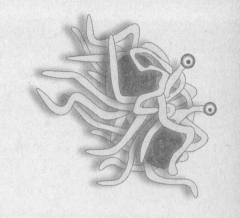

Illustration Credits

About the Author

BOBBY HENDERSON is twenty-five years old and lives in Corvallis, Oregon. He holds a B.S. in physics, and although he has received several job offers from Las Vegas gambling interests (really, we're serious), he currently supports himself as a full-time prophet. Bobby got his start as a prophet in 2005, shortly after the Flying Spaghetti Monster appeared before him and disclosed that He was the true creator of the universe. Satisfied that this was no hoax, Bobby mailed a letter to the Kansas school board in which he proposed that FSMism be taught alongside Evolution and Intelligent Design in high-school biology classes. To his great disappointment, he received no response from the school board regarding his revelation. So Bobby posted his open letter on the website www.Venganza.org (which can also be found through www.FlyingSpaghettiMonster.com), and soon he began hearing from other Pastafarians. It has been estimated that ten million people worldwide have been touched by His Noodly Appendage. *The Gospel of the Flying Spaghetti Monster* is Bobby's first religious tome.

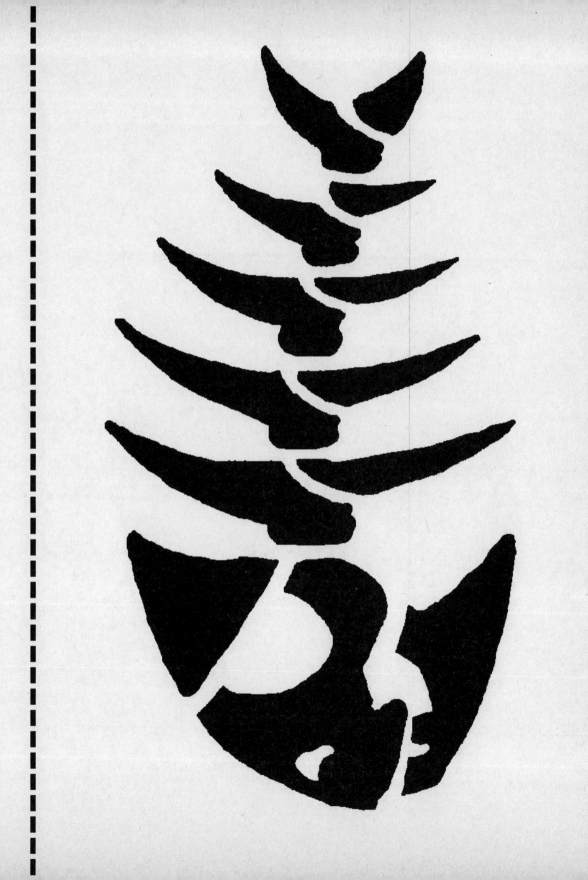

Share with a midget friend!